More
Paintbox Knits

41 New Designs for Kids

MARY H. BONNETTE

JO LYNNE MURCHLAND

of the Sassy Skein

Martingale™
& COMPANY

CREDITS

PRESIDENT · *Nancy J. Martin*
CEO · *Daniel J. Martin*
PUBLISHER · *Jane Hamada*
EDITORIAL DIRECTOR · *Mary V. Green*
MANAGING EDITOR · *Tina Cook*
TECHNICAL EDITOR · *Ursula Reikes*
COPY EDITOR · *Ellen Balstad*
DESIGN DIRECTOR · *Stan Green*
ILLUSTRATOR · *Robin Strobel*
TEXT DESIGNER · *Trina Stahl*
COVER DESIGNER · *Stan Green*
PHOTOGRAPHER · *Gloria Markel Kramer*

Martingale™
& COMPANY

More Paintbox Knits: 41 New Designs for Kids
© 2003 by Mary H. Bonnette and Jo Lynne Murchland

Martingale & Company
20205 144th Avenue NE
Woodinville, WA 98072-8478 USA
www.martingale-pub.com

Printed in China
08 07 06 05 04 03   8 7 6 5 4 3 2 1

MISSION STATEMENT

We are dedicated to providing quality products and service by working together to inspire creativity and to enrich the lives we touch.

Library of Congress Cataloging-in-Publication Data

Bonnette, Mary H.
    More paintbox knits : 41 new designs for kids /
Mary H. Bonnette, Jo Lynne Murchland.
        p.   cm.
    ISBN 1-56477-441-4
    1. Knitting—Patterns.   2. Children's clothing.
I. Murchland, Jo Lynne.   II. Title.
    TT825 .B6497 2003
    746.43'2041—dc21

                                        2002011255

DEDICATION

To the many special people who have touched our lives and inspired our work. It would be impossible to name each and every one of you.

To the three girls who continue to inspire us, Ashleigh, Rachel, and Savannah. Their passion for color and style has influenced us and has been the foundation for our Sassy Skein designs.

To Harris and Gayle, our husbands, who share their ideas and support for our labor of love. They have so graciously taken on many hats as our business has grown over the years. They have been our sounding boards, encouragers, and best critics. Now, if we could only teach them to knit!

ACKNOWLEDGMENTS

We extend our special thanks to the following people:

The yarn companies for sharing their yummy yarns with us: Cascade Yarns; Classic Elite Yarns; Dale of Norway; Patons; Russi Sales, Inc.; Skacel Collection, Inc.; S. R. Kertzer; Tahki-Stacy Charles, Inc.; and Wool in the Woods.

The button companies for the creative touch they have added to our garments: Dress It Up; Jesse James Button Co.; JHB International; LaMode; Mill Hill by Gay Bowles Sales, Inc.; Trendsetter; and Zecca.

The talented models who inspire and charm us: Savannah Bonnette, Ashleigh Cain, Rachel Cain, Callie Jones, Casey Marie Kramer, Austin Lachmann, Ainsley Lederfind, Joel Lederfind, Max Molloy, Leli Molzan, Lee Shen Molzan, Caleb Morris, and Isabelle Wolff.

The wonderful professional staff at Martingale & Company. We appreciate their support. Their faith in us has been an ongoing source of motivation. Special appreciation goes to Ursula Reikes, our technical editor!

We also wish to extend our sincere thanks to the many dedicated people who have made this project possible. Without their help and support, this book would exist only in our imagination. Gloria, our photographer, traveled over a thousand miles and spent a month on location to give us the captivating photos that appear in this book. And Leo, her able assistant and father, skillfully handled the sets and camera equipment, and at the same time, kept our models smiling. The spirit and enthusiasm that the children brought to the photo shoots was contagious and helped to relieve the hectic nature that is inevitable on such occasions. Many juice boxes, mini pizzas, and promises for later were shared. We are truly indebted to the parents, the friends, and the families who gave so freely of their valuable time and assistance to turn our vision into reality.

Contents

Pattern Pitter-Patter

THE PATTERNS IN this book were written with a child's comfort in mind. We know those squirmy little bodies dislike lumpy, bumpy seams, and tight collars and cuffs. Everything we write into a pattern we do for a reason. Often it is for the benefit of the knitter, but it is also for the comfort of the child.

Many of the garments in this book are knit in the round. There are several advantages in using this style or technique. Working with the right side of your work always facing you allows you to watch your garment take shape. And for those of you not crazy about purling, guess what? You get to knit those stitches! Also, circular knitting eliminates side seams, which is a plus for the both the knitter and the youngster.

Another feature of our patterns that we feel gives a more professional finished look to a garment is the option to knit shoulder stitches together using the three-needle bind off method. We encourage the use of this technique as a way to eliminate potentially bulky shoulder seams, and we feel that the knitter and the pint-size wearer will be pleased with the results.

All sleeves in our patterns are worked from the top down. This means you pick up stitches from the armhole edge and work toward the cuff.

We do this for two reasons. First, it is an easy way to finish an armhole and, at the same time, a sleeve. Second, it leaves a smooth and comfortable opening. There is seldom reason to give a child's garment the tailored fit of a set-in sleeve. Our style of armhole and sleeve leaves a little growing room, which moms are always happy to see. Here's a tip for knitting the first few rows of a sleeve with a 24" circular needle: Pull the flexible cable through one-third to halfway around as you work the row. Repeat this as often as you need to for the first several rows. After those initial rows, the sleeve will be loose enough that this will no longer be necessary. This little trick works anytime you are knitting in a tight spot.

In this book, most of the sleeves do not involve periodic decreasing as you work toward the cuff. Therefore, the garment will have fuller, straighter sleeves with more elbow room for the active, growing child. Sleeve decreasing is placed in the row just before the beginning of the cuff so that the cuff is more fitted to the wrist.

We determine the overall fit of our garments with their purpose in mind. For example, is it an outer garment, such as a cardigan or a jacket, that will be worn over other clothing? Or is it a short-sleeve tunic that will be worn next to the skin for a slim-looking fit? The dimensions and shape of these two types of garments are intended to be just a little different.

In determining which size garment you should make, you will need to consider several factors. For example, figure out how long you think it will take you to knit the garment. What season will it be when you finish, and does that make a difference for your project? Then consider how fast the little one you are knitting for is growing. Remember—they do grow fast! Once you answer these questions, take and record the child's measurements of the items listed below. Then use our size chart below to help you select the garment size you should make.

- Chest
- Length from back of neck to waist
- Length of arm from top of shoulder

- **For girls:** length from back of neck to hemline of choice
- Width of shoulder from center back to top of one shoulder
- Waist
- Hips
- Wrist circumference
- Neck circumference (for a comfortable neckline)
- Head circumference (You need to make sure a garment will go over a child's head and that a hat will fit.)

You will find our garments are sized and shaped to be roomy enough to let your little tyke take off and go. Pick out your favorite pattern, determine which size is right, grab your yarn and needles, and cast on!

Size	18M	2T	3T	4T	6	8	10
Chest	22"–24"	24"–26"	25"–28"	26"–30"	30"–32 1/2"	32"–35"	34"–36"
Sweater length	11"–13"	12"–14"	13"–15"	14"–16 1/2"	15"–17 1/2"	16"–18 1/2"	18"–19"
Drop sleeve	8"–9"	9"–10"	10"–11"	11"–12"	12"–14"	14"–15"	14"–16"
Short sleeve	1 1/2"–2 3/4"	2 1/2"–3"	2 3/4"–3"	3"–3 1/2"	3 3/4"–4"	4"–4 1/2"	4"–5"
Dress/jumper length	14"–15"	15 1/2"–17 1/2"	17"–19"	18"–20"	20"–22"	22"–24"	23"–26"

Use the chart as a guide to help you choose the correct size. Measurements may vary depending on the type of garment being fit.

Knitting-Bag Essentials

HAVE YOU EVER just left your favorite yarn shop with the most luscious yarn, and it is all you can do not to break out those needles and cast on as you are driving home? (Actually, one of us has been known to do just that!) Keeping a well-stocked knitting bag will help you get an immediate start on those exciting projects. We recommend you keep the following tools and supplies in your knitting bag all the time. In fact, we suggest that you have more than one bag stocked and ready. Keep one in your favorite knitting room at home for your main project, and keep another one for traveling.

Cable needle: For textured stitches, a cable needle is indispensable. If you have ever found yourself without a cable needle and have tried to substitute with things such as a pencil, a paper clip, or a straw, you know just how great a cable needle can be!

Calculator: A calculator is something our knitting bags are never without. It will come in handy in comparing your work to the pattern or in recalculating the pattern's measurements to increase or decrease stitches or rows as needed to fit your child.

Circular needles: We think that once you start using circular needles, you'll never want to put them down. Stock your bag with 24"-long circular needles in sizes 5, 6, 7, 8, 9, and 10. They are the most common sizes needed for the patterns in this book. Circular needles are also better if you knit around small children, because there is less risk of poking an inquisitive little one. Circular needles are our choice, even when we are not knitting in the round. Try it! (See "Knitting with Circular Needles" on page 11.)

Double-pointed needles: These needles are purchased in sets of four or five. We recommend stocking your bag with sizes 4, 5, and 6. You will find these useful for sock, hat, and mitten patterns.

End caps: A pair of end caps is useful for keeping your work from sliding off your needles accidentally while your project is tucked away in your knitting bag.

Gauge ruler: Measuring your knitting gauge is important to ensure that your garment comes out the size specified by the pattern you are following. Use a gauge ruler so that you can measure your stitches and rows accurately.

Graph paper: We find graph paper helpful to visualize color changes and stitches for a complex pattern, make up our own graphed design, or draw a quick design. You can find small spiral graph-paper notebooks in most bookstores. Storing one of these in your bag is a great way to keep up with your notes, measurements, and graphed designs!

Pencils: Consider keeping a mechanical pencil or two in your bag for jotting down notes and sketching. And they won't inadvertently leave a mark on the project in your bag.

Row counter: Patterns will sometimes call for keeping track of rows. A row counter is an easy way to count the rows you've worked.

Scissors: A small but essential item!

Size F or G crochet hook: Either one of these medium-sized crochet hooks is great for adding a single-crochet edge to hems or for creating chains for things such as drawstrings and button loops.

Small notebook: A small notebook is important to keep track of things such as your measurements, any revisions you may have made, and yarn amounts and dye lots. Later, you will be happy you kept all the information in one easy-to-retrieve place.

Stitch holders: For almost any garment, you will need to place neckline or shoulder stitches on a stitch holder until you can knit the shoulder seams together or pick up stitches for the neck ribbing. For most projects, you will need at least three stitch holders, 3" to 4" long.

Stitch markers: Using stitch markers as you knit makes it easy to keep track of stitches visually. It can also keep you from having to continually count and recount your stitches.

Tape measure: Taking measurements of the child you are knitting for and measuring the garment as you knit are both keys to a well-fitting garment.

Tapestry needle (sharp or pointed needle): This needle is well-suited for embroidery or embellishment work.

Yarn needle (blunt-ended needle): This needle is perfect for joining seams, sewing on pockets, securing buttons, and weaving in yarn ends.

Zippered pouch: We recommend using a small zippered pouch—a clear one is best—to hold little items in your knitting bag. It will keep them all together and easy to find, and it will prevent them from catching or snagging your yarn.

Selecting Yarns

WE HAVE CHOSEN a variety of yarns for the model garments in this book based on the features of each garment. For example, for little girls' dresses, which are worn next to the skin and should drape nicely, we chose DK-weight cotton yarns. Bulkier outer garments intended to keep little children warm are knit in worsted weight or bulky weight wools. Throughout this book, we provide you with specific information regarding each yarn used, along with actual color numbers or descriptions. But remember, these are only suggestions. We work closely with each yarn company to ensure that the yarns we use will be available for a long time, but obviously yarns and colors come and go. And not all yarn shops are able to carry all yarns or all colors. Please feel free to substitute your own color choices or your favorite yarns. Don't let a lack of availability of a yarn or a color stop you from knitting a pattern you fall in love with.

Choose your own yarns. Your climate may dictate the use of a cotton yarn instead of wool, or your granddaughter's favorite color just might be purple! Whatever yarns you do use, please take the time to make a gauge swatch. Differences in fiber content may give you many different looks, but a difference in stitch gauge will give you a different size. Spending a few minutes to check your gauge in the beginning may save you hours later when you realize you should have made an adjustment in needle size to get the proper stitch gauge—and the proper fit! If you use the same yarn for the gauge swatch as for the garment, use it to test the launderability and colorfastness of the yarn. Be sure to read the manufacturer's label for washing and care instructions.

As a general rule, when the discussion slips into yarn jargon, keep the following information in mind.

Yarn	Needle Size	Sts/4"
Fingering yarn	1–4 needles	26–32 sts = 4"
Sport yarn	4–6 needles	23–25 sts = 4"
DK yarn	5–6 needles	21–22 sts = 4"
Worsted yarn	5–8 needles	17–21 sts = 4"
Bulky/ chunky yarn	9–17 needles	8–16 sts = 4"

Knitting with Circular Needles

WHEN KNITTING FOR children, circular needles have several advantages. First, knitting with them eliminates the need for side seams, making the garments more comfortable for those little bodies. And no side seams also means one less finishing step. Let's face it, sewing seams together is no one's favorite part of knitting.

Second, knitting with circular needles is actually faster than using straight needles because circular needles are lightweight and not as cumbersome as straight needles. For fast knitting, we like Addi Turbo needles. The yarn slides beautifully along these needles. For slip-stitch knitting, you might want to try bamboo circular needles. The yarn doesn't slide quite as easily on bamboo, which is actually a timesaving advantage for slip-stitch patterns. Your yarn is less likely to slip off the needle as you try to slip the correct stitches back and forth. Bamboo needles, unlike metal needles, feel smooth and warm in your hands while you work.

A third advantage of knitting with circular needles is that the right side of your work is always facing you. This allows you to create a stockinette stitch by knitting every row rather than using the traditional method of knitting one row and purling the next. Not only can you knit the majority of stitches, which most people prefer to do, but you can also always see the right side of your work. This is helpful in keeping track of your pattern and color changes and in visualizing your garment's size and shape. Seeing your garment take shape is both exciting and satisfying.

Another advantage is that you can use circular needles to knit back and forth without the awkwardness of having to turn your work at the end of every row. This is especially helpful if you are working with multicolored stripes. And because they are so lightweight and flexible, circular needles are easier on your wrists. You might find your hands and wrists don't fatigue as quickly when using circular needles.

Circular needles are available in lengths from 11" to 60". When knitting children's garments, we feel a 24"-long circular needle works well even for small spaces such as armholes and collars. You can pull the flexible cable through groups of stitches, allowing you to easily work these small areas. You can also always use two circulars just like two straight needles, but with a lot more bend and curve if you are working an area such as a small neckline. Place end caps on the needle ends not in use, and away you go. Because circular needles are so lightweight and flexible, they are easy to pack and take in your knitting bag. Give circular knitting a try! At least give circular needles a try! We think you will agree that they are fast, fun, and easy.

Back to Basics

GAUGE SWATCH

HAVE YOU ever accused a loved one of wasting time because he or she wouldn't take those few minutes to stop and ask for directions? Well, not making a gauge swatch before you start a project could be the knitting counterpart to this all-too-familiar scenario.

Knitting a gauge swatch really is a time-saver in the long run. To make it properly, you should knit a 5" x 5" square in the main pattern stitch for your project. When finished, lay it out smoothly. Using a stitch gauge, count the stitches and the rows in a 4" section. If the number of stitches and rows matches the pattern, start knitting. If you have more stitches and rows, you are knitting too tightly; try a larger-sized needle. If you have less stitches and rows, you are knitting too loosely; try a smaller-sized needle.

While knitting your garment, check your gauge again after you have knit several inches. Sometimes people knit more tightly or loosely when they have a needle full of stitches.

THREE-NEEDLE SHOULDER SEAM BIND OFF (3-Needle BO)

IN MOST patterns, the "BO sts" (bind off stitches) instruction is given at the completion of the back and front sections of a garment. The unspoken technique on how to accomplish the bind off is left up to the expertise of you, the knitter. In so many instances, BO simply means passing one stitch over the other until all stitches have been worked off the needle. And this does work, except that you still have to seam these ends together. The finishing aspects of a garment are so important, and here is one place where you can always present the look of an expert knitter. If you only learn one new thing with every project you do, let the three-needle method of joining shoulders be one of them!

When you are instructed to "BO sts," place these stitches on a stitch holder and leave a long tail of yarn to work with later. When you complete the back and front, transfer the back stitches onto one needle and the front stitches onto a second needle. Hold them with right sides together and make sure the needle tips are going in the same direction. With a third needle and the yarn tail, knit the first stitch on each needle together as one stitch. Repeat for the second stitches on each needle. Pass the first stitch worked over the second stitch worked and drop off the end of the right-hand needle. Continue to knit one stitch from each needle together; then pass the first stitch over the second, until only one stitch remains on the needle. Pull the tail of yarn through this stitch to secure. You end up with a perfect shoulder seam every time. Master it!

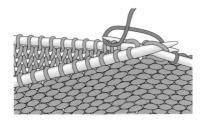

BUTTONHOLES

CHILDREN CAN be good barometers of how well a garment accommodates their idea of comfort. They are rarely happy about tight necks, bulky shoulder seams, or the wrestling match that can take place while getting them dressed.

Well-placed buttonholes can be the magic element that allows your labor of love to become your little one's favorite garment. Consider the possibilities—buttons at the shoulders for sweaters or sundresses, buttons down the front for plackets or cardigans, buttons down one or both sides for easy access or just for effect, or even buttons down the back so that the child can't take the garment off! Buttonholes can be the key to a successful fit, but they need to be sturdy and kid friendly for buttoning because, in time, every child wants to "do it myself."

Methods for making buttonholes abound. The method you choose will depend on your level of expertise, your personal preference, or the look that you are trying to achieve. The following three sections introduce a few of the standard methods for making buttonholes; the fourth section covers buttonhole spacing. As you work, remember to place buttonholes for boys on the left side and buttonholes for girls on the right side. For some of the unisex garments in this book, the buttonholes may be on the wrong side for the child.

Knit 2 Together, Yarn Over (K2tog, YO)
This is the easiest method for making buttonholes and the one mentioned most often. It is wise to

reinforce this buttonhole with a single-crochet stitch around the opening so that the "do-it-myself" child doesn't stretch it out. For beginning knitters, this method may solve the panic that sets in when their skills are limited.

Work to the placement of the first buttonhole on the button band, knit 2 together, and then yarn over, which means to wrap the yarn around the needle one time. The yarn over replaces the decrease from the knit 2 together so that the total stitches on the button band remain the same. Continue working the button band, repeating the "knit 2 together, yarn over" as needed for the desired number of buttonholes.

One-Row Horizontal
This method will give you a buttonhole that is strong and well defined. This is especially good if your button is decorative or larger than ½" in diameter.

1. Work as instructed to first buttonhole. Bring working yarn to front, slip next stitch as if to purl, and return yarn to back of work.

2. *Slip next stitch from left needle to right needle, pass first slipped stitch over second slipped stitch, and drop it off end of needle. Repeat from * once, twice, or three times, depending on the size of the buttonhole you need. Slip the last stitch on right needle back to left needle and turn your work.

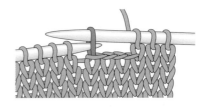

3. Cast on stitches using the cable cast-on method as follows. With wrong side of work facing, move yarn to back of work, *insert right needle between first and second stitches on left needle, draw up a loop from yarn at back of work, and place it on left-hand needle. Repeat from * once, twice, or as many times as

needed to replace stitches bound off in step 2, plus one additional stitch. Turn your work.

4. With right side facing and yarn in back, slip first stitch from left needle to right needle; then pass the extra cast-on stitch over it to close the buttonhole. You will now have the original stitch count to proceed as instructed by the pattern. The first stitch on the left-hand needle is stitch 1 of the stitch count toward the next buttonhole.

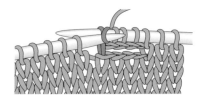

Two-Row Horizontal

This method will create a buttonhole that has a very similar look to the one-row horizontal. This two-row technique also creates a neat, sturdy buttonhole that will maintain its shape with use.

1. On button band, work to placement of buttonhole. For a 4-stitch buttonhole, *knit 2 stitches, then with left needle, slip first stitch over second stitch, and drop off of needle. Repeat from * 3 times—4 stitches bound off. Continue working across button band, repeating from * for each buttonhole.

2. On next row, *work to within 1 stitch of bound-off stitches. Work into front and back of next stitch to increase 1 stitch. Cast on 3 stitches (1 less than the number of bound-off stitches) using the cable cast-on method as

described above. Continue working across button band, repeating from * for each buttonhole.

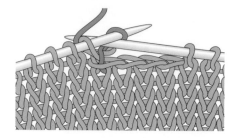

After working into front and back of stitch, turn work and cast on 3 stitches.

3. On next row, work cast-on stitches through the back loop to tighten them for a neater look.

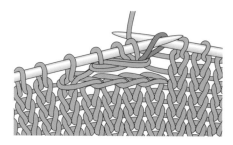

Work cast-on stitches through the back loop.

Spacing

The pattern directions will often say "space X-number buttonholes evenly on button band." Spacing buttonholes evenly can be an intimidating challenge for a beginning knitter or even for an experienced knitter who has been knitting afghans over a lifetime. However, it is just a simple math problem. Refer to the following example to see how it's done.

Let's say your garment size requires 5 buttons and you will be working on 67 stitches. You've already purchased the buttons and know that you need a 3-stitch buttonhole to accommodate the size of each button. That means you'll need 15 stitches (3 stitches x 5 buttons) of the button band to work the buttonholes. It is best to place the top and bottom buttons 2 or possibly 3 stitches in from their respective edges. Let's do the math on a 67-stitch button band:

- Leaving 2 stitches each at top and bottom = 4 stitches
- 5 buttonholes with 3 stitches each = 15 stitches
- Total stitches needed to this point = 19 stitches
- Total stitches remaining = 48 stitches
- Placing 3 buttonholes between top and bottom buttonholes on button band will create 4 spaces between buttonholes.
- 48 remaining stitches ÷ 4 spaces = 12 stitches in each space

The sequence for spacing 5 buttonholes evenly on a 67-stitch button band will be 2 stitches from the top, *3 stitches for buttonhole, 12 stitches for space. Repeat from * 3 times; then add 3 stitches for the last buttonhole and 2 stitches to bottom edge to equal 67 stitches.

Before picking up stitches for a button band, work out the math using the number of stitches as instructed in the pattern. You may find, based on the number of stitches you will use for each buttonhole, that you need to adjust the number of stitches to be picked up by a stitch or two. Do not adjust more than one or two stitches, however; otherwise, you will definitely change the fit of the button band.

PICKING UP STITCHES

UNLESS INSTRUCTED otherwise, always pick up stitches with the right side of the garment facing you. Using the right-hand needle, insert the tip of the needle into the hole between the first and second stitch, wrap yarn around needle, and pull the loop through the hole to the right side. Continue in the same manner until you have the required number of stitches as specified in your pattern.

READING GRAPHS

THE EXTRA little touch of a small design will add so much to your child's garment. One of the great things about making children's wear is that you are not stuck with a tedious design that can wear you out long before the garment is finished. For the most part, borders and flecks of color here and there are sufficient to make your garment come alive. It is definitely worth the effort to have some basic knowledge about reading graphs.

Because we knit from the bottom up (on most occasions), graphs are represented in the order in which they are worked unless otherwise indicated. On right side or odd-numbered rows, read a graph from right to left; on wrong side or even-numbered rows, read from left to right. The color key, or the stitch key when necessary, will contain the information needed to insert the design into your garment. Take the time to understand what the graph shows regarding design placement and number of repeats.

BLOCKING OPTIONS AND GARMENT CARE

BLOCKING METHODS will vary according to the fiber content and the stitch content of your garment. Because children's garments generally are made with more durable yarns such as cotton, wool, or blends, you will not need to be concerned about how to handle flashy novelty fibers that are so popular at your local yarn shop.

Generally speaking, blocking is high on the list of finishing techniques that give your garment a more finished look. Depending on the fiber content, some garments respond to very light steaming and others may require soaking in a tub of cold water for 15 to 20 minutes. Yarns with some elasticity, such as wool or wool blends, respond well to a light amount of steam; cottons and mixed yarns can be moistened with a little more gusto. It's a good idea to test the colorfastness of the yarn before blocking; use your gauge swatch for this test. Before you do anything, however, check the band on your ball of yarn. It will give specific information as to the handling and care recommended by the manufacturer.

To steam block, turn the garment wrong side out, set the iron to the low steam setting, and hold the iron approximately 1" to 2" above the garment to allow the steam to penetrate the fibers. Do not place the iron directly on a garment or you could irreversibly damage the fiber. Use a top-to-bottom motion with the iron on the front; then flip the garment over and repeat on the back. Cover a padded flat surface with a towel. Turn the garment right side out, hand shape, and pin to the padded surface. Allow the garment to dry completely in a cool, dry area.

For straighter fibers, such as cotton or mixed blends, you can use more moisture to block the garment. Position and pin your garment to a padded surface and spray it with cool water. If your garment has heavy texturing, ribs, or cables, you can actually get it quite moist. Take great care not to stretch any ribbing or flatten out the design before spraying. Allow the garment to dry completely in a cool, dry area before moving it. The garment shaping will be retained.

You can also use a tub for blocking. Immerse the garment completely in cool water, wrap it in a large towel, and squeeze without twisting. If necessary, repeat the process with a second towel. Many knitters prefer using the spin cycle on the washing machine instead of having two soggy towels. Try the gentle cycle and place a regular-size towel in with the garment. This will help balance the spin process and also help absorb some of the water. Like the other methods, lay the garment out on a flat surface away from sunlight, shape and pin it to size, and let it dry thoroughly.

When it is wash day and the favorite treasured garment is covered with chocolate and dumped on the laundry room floor, and the 800-number to Heloise is lost, what's a parent to do? You can help prevent laundry worries with a little planning before you make the garment. When deciding on a yarn, it's a good idea to anticipate the garment's intended use. Ideally, select rugged fibers that will withstand the washing machine. Reserve more delicate fibers for garments that are kept for special occasions. Yarn shops are full of wonderful cottons, blends, washable wools, and acrylics, so choose wisely for the child's garment.

If possible, stains should be spot washed as soon as possible and chlorine bleach should be avoided. The longer the spot lingers in the fiber, the harder it will be to get out. Cool water and mild soap are preferable for all garments, especially those with multiple colors. The colorfast properties should be tested before the garment is plunged into a full tub of water. Whether it is washed by hand or machine washed on the gentle cycle, the garment should be dried on a towel away from sunlight and any artificial heat source.

Proper care and storage will keep a garment in good condition for years to come. It will be a hand-me-down that another child could wear with pride. So be sure that the garment is preserved in a protective, ventilated bag or storage box. It should be folded carefully (never hung on a hanger), wrapped in acid-free tissue paper, placed in a proper storage container, and stored at room temperature. By following these steps, the garment will always be ready for use.

Knitting Techniques

A WELL-STOCKED knitter's library may have volumes of books dedicated to each of these techniques. It is not our intent to write a research book on the subject. However, we would be remiss in not including the various techniques that you will encounter as you knit garments from this book. What follows is a brief analysis of certain design features that are included in our patterns. It is intended to make you feel comfortable about taking on a new challenge and to assure you that none of this is as complex as it may look. This may be your opportunity to apply what is considered an adult technique to a child's garment. So plunge in for what could be a new adventure!

CABLES AND TWISTS

IN MANY cases, the cable and twist techniques have a very similar look. They appear in a design as stitches that cross or weave through a pattern. They also share the basic premise of knitting stitches out of sequence. There are endless possibilities and combinations of stitches that will satisfy even the most adventuresome knitter. The effect is instantly appreciated, and you will not believe how easily you can make an impact on a design.

Cables

You will need a cable needle for this technique. Check with your yarn supply source; there is more than one kind of cable needle. To make a cable "cross," put a specified number of stitches on a cable needle and hold them in back or in front of your work. Work a specified number of stitches from the left needle to the right needle. Then work the stitches off the cable needle. Holding stitches on the cable needle at the back of your work will result in a left to right cross. For a right to left cross, hold stitches on the cable needle at the front of your work. Combinations of this simple technique can put interest and texture in an otherwise ordinary pattern. Refer to "Classy Cables Pullover with Hat" (page 43) for an elementary use of the cable technique.

Twists

Working a twist pattern does not require a cable needle even though the stitches are shifted to a different placement in the knitting order. These stitch patterns are often referred to as mock cables because, in most instances, they look similar to a cable stitch. To work a basic twist, slip a number of stitches from the left needle to the right needle, work a specified number of stitches on the left needle and slip them back to the left needle, and then go back and work the slipped stitches. There are right twists and left twists; their direction depends on the order in which the stitches are worked. The twisting and drawing of stitches together will make a garment more dense. Be sure to check the stitch gauge of your pattern. Refer to "Tickle Me Pink Pullover" (page 61), "Slip, Slide, and Twist Cardigan with Hat" (page 102), and "Trim the Tree Pullover" (page 107) for examples of this technique.

ENTRELAC

An entrelac garment appears to be a woven basket of diagonally knitted strips of yarn. There is a definite three-dimensional, intricate look to this distinctive knitting style. The entrelac technique holds a unique place in a knitter's repertoire. It is a relatively easy technique because you work only with a few stitches at a time. From right-sloping rectangles to left-sloping rectangles, the progression of the design across the needle involves picking up stitches and decreasing stitches. Your pattern will designate the number of stitches per block, and there will be twice the number of rows as stitches. Each block of stitches remains on the needle as you move on to the next set of working stitches.

Of all the knitting techniques, this one encourages you to be most creative. Because of its woven nature, there can be endless variations on a theme and you can introduce a little variety without having to carry it throughout the whole garment. The triangles and rectangles can be a blank canvas for your imagination. You can use different textured stitches, cables, colors, intarsia designs, or whatever strikes you. Refer to "Festive Fella Pullover" (page 33) and "Swiss Miss Pullover with Scarf" (page 37) for garments using this technique.

FAIR ISLE COLOR WORK

A principle component of Fair Isle knitting is that the garment is usually worked in stockinette stitch, with at least two colors being worked in a row. On a right-side row, both colors are stranded or carried across the row on the back side of the garment. On wrong-side rows, the yarn is carried on the front side of the garment.

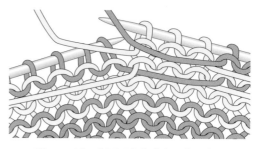

Wrong side of Fair Isle knitting showing colors carried across the rows.

This technique often includes graphed designs that are repeated many times across a row. The colors may change as you work the graphed pattern, and in some cases, more than two colors may be used.

The colorful garments that use the Fair Isle technique are quite recognizable, great conversation pieces, and always popular. It is easy to be charmed by their accents of color and attention to small details. While whole garments can be made with Fair Isle and there are many, many books on the subject, for this book, the use of Fair Isle is simply a decorative way to make an interesting border, sleeve design, or shoulder treatment. Refer to "Rush Hour Cardigan" (page 80), "Merry-Go-Round Pullover" (page 93), and "Acorns Dress" (page 124) for examples of this technique.

INTARSIA COLOR WORK

Intarsia differs from Fair Isle inasmuch as this technique creates a self-contained pattern. An intarsia design is graphed or charted and placed in a garment, and it features a particular motif, picture, or abstract pattern. Often there are many colors involved in the design, and these colors need to be linked and stranded on the wrong side of the garment. One of the keys to a well done intarsia design is to organize the various colors on the wrong side. Balls of yarn can get jumbled up easily in just a few rows, so they should be moved in the order they are used. To keep clutter to a minimum, you can also wind bobbins with the different colors for small design areas or cut long strands of the various colors and let them hang freely in the back.

One important component of working this technique is to link one yarn color to the next color being worked. Proper linking will eliminate unattractive holes and give you the desired result. When you work to the color change, pick up the new color under and then over the dropped yarn; repeat for every change of color.

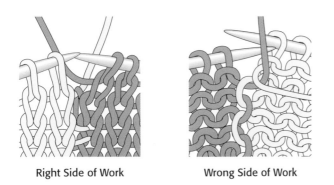

Right Side of Work   Wrong Side of Work

The tension on the yarn that is carried in the back is another important component to a well-done intarsia design. In the patterns, you will see the phrase "carry yarn loosely in the back." This may sound like an easy request, but you may find that you will have to make a conscious effort to leave plenty of give in the carried yarn. This will allow the pattern stitches to relax in their intended space without being distorted by the tension on the wrong side of the garment. Refer to "Swiss Miss Pullover with Scarf" (page 37) and "Cat Tales Cardigan" (page 87) for examples of intarsia.

SLIP STITCH

THIS TECHNIQUE may be the easiest of all. What could be simpler than moving a stitch from one needle to another without doing anything to it— just slipping? Slip-stitch patterns work only one color at a time in a row. By working rows of different colors and slipping stitches on the needle that have the color of the preceding row, a pattern evolves that does not require carrying yarn, linking colors, or untangling bobbins.

There are some rules to follow when working with the slip-stitch technique. All stitches are slipped purlwise on the right side of your garment unless instructed otherwise. The wrong side is usually a purl row. See—we told you this was easy! You will also use a circular needle because the pattern may instruct you to work two consecutive rows from the right-side position. To do this, slide the stitches to the other end of the needle to be in position to knit the second right-side row. Also, if you are working multiple colors, it may be necessary to slide the stitches to the end of the needle that has the yarn color you will need to pick up. This technique is a fast and easy way to mix a lot of color into a garment. When worked in a single color, this technique can quickly give texture and density.

If someone wants very intricate and intense slip-stitch patterns with charts that will make their eyes cross, they will find many in the marketplace. However, to make a wonderful, colorful child's garment, it is not necessary to get this involved. Therefore, the patterns in this book that use the slip-stitch technique are not charted. Simple row-by-row, written instructions are sufficient.

If you want to keep things uncomplicated and have an unlimited opportunity to work with color, slip-stitch patterns are for you. You get a lot of bang for your buck! Try "Tri-Color Tweed Pullover" (page 30), "Swiss Miss Pullover with Scarf" (page 37), "Rush Hour Cardigan" (page 80), "Slip, Slide, and Twist Cardigan with Hat" (page 102), "Harvest Moon Cardigan with Pants" (page 119), and "Ja Makin' Me Crazy Dress" (page 127) to test this technique.

STITCHES

THERE ARE some stitches that are repeated often throughout the projects in this book. It seems safe to assume that you are familiar with most of them. What follows is a very brief explanation of how to knit them so that every knitter can start with the same level of knowledge. Pattern stitches that apply to a specific project are described in detail in the project's instructions.

Stockinette Stitch (St st)
Any number of stitches

Row 1 (RS): Knit.
Row 2 (WS): Purl.
Rep rows 1 and 2.

Reverse Stockinette Stitch (Rev St st)
Any number of stitches

Row 1 (RS): Purl.
Row 2 (WS): Knit.
Rep rows 1 and 2.

Garter Stitch
Any number of stitches

Knit all right side and wrong side rows.

Seed Stitch
Any number of stitches

Row 1 (RS): *K1, P1, rep from * across row.
Row 2 (WS): Knit the purl sts and purl the knit sts as they face you.
Rep rows 1 and 2.

Double Moss Stitch
Even number of stitches

Rows 1 and 2: *K2, P2, rep from * across row.
Rows 3 and 4: *P2, K2, rep from * across row.
Rep rows 1–4.

Crochet Chain

Make a slipknot and place it on the hook. Wrap the yarn over the hook and draw it through the loop of the slipknot. Continue to wrap the yarn over the hook and draw it through the last loop formed.

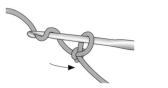

Wrap yarn over hook and pull through loop.

Repeat, forming as many chain stitches as desired.

EDGING

Single Crochet

Working from right to left, insert the crochet hook into the first edge stitch, draw up a loop, wrap the yarn over the hook, and pull this loop through the first loop. *Insert the crochet hook into the next stitch, wrap yarn over the hook, pull this loop through to front, wrap yarn over hook, and pull this loop through both loops. Repeat from * until the bound-off edge has been covered.

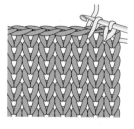
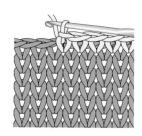

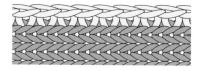

Picot or Hem

This is a very attractive edging for sleeves, necks, and hemlines, and it is simple to do. A picot edging is a hemmed edging. Finishing instructions are included in each appropriate pattern.

In stockinette stitch, work the number of rows specified for the depth of the hem, ending on WS row. If working on an even number of stitches, work the next row as follows: K2, *YO, K2tog; rep from * to end of row. For an odd number of stitches, work as follows: K1, *YO, K2tog; rep from * to end. Now work in stockinette stitch for the same number of rows that preceded the picot row. When garment is complete, turn the hem under to the wrong side of the garment at the YO row. Lay the hem flat against the garment and sew down to the wrong side.

Baby Cable Ribbing
Multiple of 4 sts plus 2

This is a decorative substitute for the traditional K2, P2 ribbing.

Row 1 (WS): K2, *P2, K2, rep from * to end.
Row 2 (RS): P2, *K2, P2, rep from * to end.
Row 3: Rep row 1.
Row 4: P2, *K2tog, and leave on needle. Insert right-hand needle between the 2 sts just knitted together. Knit the first st again. Slide both sts from needle together; P2, rep from * to end.
Rep rows 1–4.

Ruffled

The projects that include ruffled edges have detailed instructions within the patterns. Ruffles give a dressy quality to any garment to which they are applied, and they are a very easy technique to work. They usually require increasing or decreasing as much as two to three times the number of stitches that you begin with.

Rolled

This edge has a relaxed and casual look. It is truly a no-brainer. There are many versions of this edge, but they all look similar and roll to the outside edge. Necklines, sleeves, and garment bottoms can all benefit from this easy technique.

Once you are ready to begin the edging, work from the right side of the garment. For hems, neck, or cuffs, work rows or rounds as directed in the pattern. BO stitches loosely so that the edge is relaxed enough to roll over to the outside. The row amounts are approximate. Yarns vary in weight and stitch gauge, and these differences can affect how many rows are needed to achieve the desired look.

I-CORD

THE OLD, empty spools of thread with tacks on top are alive and well in today's knitting world. The only difference is that we now work the same magic on a double-pointed knitting needle. The I-cord technique has many uses for a knitted garment. For example, it can be used as an embellishment, it can be worked as an attached edging for a neckline, or it can be used as a fancy drawstring to hold up your britches. As a drawstring, it is simple to make and has more substance than the usual crocheted chain.

Beginning with your double-pointed needles or a circular needle, cast on 2, 3, or 4 stitches. The pattern will tell you how many stitches to cast on. After cast on, do not turn. Slide the stitches to the other end of the needle, keep the yarn in the back of the needle, pull or bring the yarn behind and across the back of the stitches, and knit the stitches that were moved to the working end of the needle. Again, do not turn. Slide the stitches to the end of the needle, with yarn in back, and knit stitches again. Repeat this process until you reach the indicated length for the pattern.

Embellishments

BUTTONS

ONE OF the easiest ways to give even the most basic of sweaters a unique and personalized look is to dress it up with buttons. Buttons can add an extra special touch that sets a garment apart from the ordinary.

In addition to serving the functional purpose of closing a garment, such as on a cardigan, buttons can be used on the front of a pullover to add a fun or festive look, like in our "Trim the Tree Pullover" (page 107) for Christmas. When used as embellishments like the ones on the tree sweater, buttons can simply be pinned on with a small safety pin. For very small children, however, we recommend you tie the buttons on from the wrong side with a piece of yarn or ribbon. This way you can remove them easily for laundering, or switch them with other buttons to give the sweater a new look!

Buttons can also be used to close shoulders, which gives a garment extra head room. If getting sweaters over the child's head is difficult, you may want to consider incorporating this idea into at least one of the shoulder seams.

Overlap and button shoulder straps of jumpers in place rather than sew shoulder seams. This way, as the youngster grows, the garment can be let down a little.

Buttons can add a colorful touch to the side seams of a garment as well. Take a look at "Ja Makin' Me Crazy Dress" (page 127). Not only is this a cute look, but it also eliminates the need to sew those side seams together.

The use of a single button can add an element of fashion to a garment such as "Merry-Go-Round Pullover" (page 93), turning the sweater into a pullover. Keep in mind that just because you add a button doesn't mean you have to make a buttonhole!

EMBROIDERY

A CREATIVE, nonknitting way to add color and interest to a garment is to embellish with embroidery stitches. Simple embroidery stitches such as the lazy daisy stitch with French knots, and the

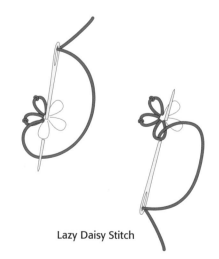

Lazy Daisy Stitch

stem stitch, can enhance any garment. See "Picket Fence Tunic" (page 74).

It is best to work the embroidery after the garment is complete and blocked. Lay the area to be worked on a flat surface. Do not stretch it or use an embroidery hoop. Use yarn and a tapestry needle to work the design onto the garment, carefully carrying the yarn loosely on the wrong side. Weave in the ends carefully.

Wrap yarn around needle two or more times.   Insert yarn close to emerging point.   French Knot

Stem Stitch

Dos and Don'ts

DO

- Buy a good-quality yarn.
- Check the stitch gauge and do what you have to do to get it right.
- Read the care instructions on the yarn label.
- Wash the gauge swatch to check for shrinkage, stretching, and color bleeding.
- Feel free to select a color palette that reflects your style; be creative.
- Adjust the length of the garment, sleeve, or collar to suit your needs.
- Adjust yarn requirements if you make changes to a pattern.
- Measure the child, and then knit the garment with future growth in mind; ease and comfort are vital.
- Embellish garments with buttons, ribbons, or doodads—kids love them!
- Carry yarn on back side of garments loosely when working multicolor designs.
- Keep it simple when given a choice.
- Complete the garment, which will be worn with pride.

DON'T

- Assume all cottons and wools are interchangeable; stitch gauges often vary, even in similar fibers.
- Use exotic yarns for children; they're too expensive and too itchy.
- Think you are knitting for a miniature adult; kids have entirely different proportions.
- Stop after making one garment. Try others to expand your expertise.
- Assume knitwear is just for cold weather.
- Launder special buttons; remove them before washing the garment.
- Bind off necklines or sleeves too tightly.
- Use chlorine bleach or other harsh chemicals for spots and stains.
- Get bogged down. Help is as close as your local yarn shop or Internet source.

Piñata Pullover with Socks

𝓕un, festive, and ready for a party, "Piñata Pullover" is perfect for any gal going to a celebration. The coordinating socks will make her toes twinkle and dance.

Pullover

GAUGE

24 STITCHES and 28 rows = 4" in pattern stitch. To save time, always check your gauge. If necessary, change needle size to obtain the correct gauge.

BODY

THIS SWEATER is knit in the round. With color A, CO 146 (158, 180) sts. Work checkerboard patt as follows:

Rnd 1: Purl.

Rnds 2 and 3: *K2 in color A, K2 in color B, rep from * around.

Rnds 4 and 5: *K2 in color B, K2 in color A, rep from * around.

Rnds 6 and 7: Rep rnds 2 and 3.

Rnds 8 and 9: Rep rnds 4 and 5.

Beg stripe color rnds:

Rnds 10–13: Color C, knit.

Rnd 14: Color D, *K1, P1, rep from * around.

Rnd 15: Color D, knit.

Rnds 16–18: Color E, knit.

Rnd 19: Color A, knit.

Rnds 20 and 21: Color F, knit.

Rnd 22: *K2 in color C, K2 in color F, rep from * around.

Rnds 23 and 24: Color F, knit.

Rnd 25: Color A, knit.

Rnds 26–30: Color D, knit.

Rnds 31 and 32: Color G, knit.

Rnd 33: Color E, *K1, P1, rep from * around.

Rnds 34–36: Color A, knit.

Rnds 37–40: Color C, knit.

Rnd 41: Color F, *K1, sl 1 (color C), rep from * around.

Rnds 42–44: Color F, knit.

Rnds 45–50: Color E, knit.

Rnds 51 and 52: Color A, knit.

Rnd 53: Color B, knit.

Rnd 54: Color A, knit.

Rnd 55: Color B, knit.

Rnd 56: Color A, knit.

Rnd 57: Color B, knit.

Rnds 58–60: Color A, knit.

This pattern is sized 2T (4T, 6).

●

FINISHED MEASUREMENTS

Chest: 24 (26, 30)"
Tunic Length: 13½ (15, 16½)"
Drop Sleeve: 10 (12, 14)"

MATERIALS

- Patons Grace, 50-gram skeins (136 yds), 100% cotton, 1 skein each of the foll colors for all sizes:

  Color A: 60040 Night (black)
  Color B: 60005 Snow (white)
  Color C: 60438 Fuchsia
  Color D: 60712 Lime
  Color E: 60625 Sungold
  Color F: 60134 Royal
  Color G: 60724 Teal

- Size 6 circular needle (24")
- Stitch holders
- Medium crochet hook
- Yarn needle

Rnds 61 and 62: Color G, knit.

Rnd 63: Color C, *K1, P1, rep from * around. Divide sts for back and front. Place back 73 (79, 90) sts on st holder. Work front 73 (79, 90) sts in St st in stripe patt as follows:

Color C: 3 (5, 7) rows. Beg with purl row.

Color D: 2 rows.

Color F: 3 rows (knit 2 rows to create garter st row, then purl 1 row).

Next row: *K1 in color F, K1 in color A, rep from * across.

Color A: 1 row.

Color E: 2 rows.

Color G: 4 (6, 8) rows.

Color C: *K1, P1, rep from * across.

Color C: 2 rows.

Color E: 2 rows.

Next row: *K4 in color E, K1 in color E, rep from * across.

Color E: 2 rows.

Color C: 3 rows.

Color F: 1 row.

Color D: *K1, P1, rep from * across.

Color D: 3 (5, 7) rows. Beg front neck and shoulder shaping.

BACK

PU STS from st holder and work same as front, omitting front neck shaping, until garment measures 13½ (15, 16½)". BO 20 (22, 25) sts for each shoulder or place on st holder for 3-needle BO, place ctr 33 (35, 40) sts on st holder. Join front and back shoulders.

FRONT NECK AND SHOULDER SHAPING

WITH RS facing, work across 25 (27, 30) sts. Place ctr 23 (25, 30) sts on st holder. Join second ball of yarn and work across rem 25 (27, 30) sts. Work both shoulders in St st foll color sequence below, dec 1 st at neck edge every row 5 times.

Color A: 3 (3, 4) rows.

Color B: 3 (3, 4) rows.

Color C: 1 row.

Color F: 5 (5, 7) rows.

BO 20 (22, 25) sts for each shoulder or place on st holder for 3-needle BO.

SLEEVES

Make 2.

SLEEVES ARE knit from the top down. They are not knit in the round, but we recommend using a circular needle. Place markers 4½ (5, 5)" from shoulder seam on front and back. With RS facing and color F, PU 56 (62, 62) sts evenly between markers. Work in St st in stripe patt.

Color F: 6 (7, 8) rows.

Color C: 1 row.

Color B: 3 rows.

Color A: 3 rows.

Color D: 4 (5, 6) rows.

Color F: *K1, P1, rep from * across.

Color C: 3 rows.

Color E: 2 rows.

Next row: Work *4 sts of color E, 1 st of color C, rep from * across.

Color E: 2 rows.

Color C: 3 rows.

Color G: *K1, P1, rep from * across.

Color G: 2 (4, 6) rows.

Color E: 1 (2, 3) rows.

Color A: 1 row.

Color F: *Work 1 st, sl 1 (color A), rep from * across.

Color F: 3 rows (knit 2 rows to create garter st row, then purl 1 row).

Cont in St st:

Color D: 2 rows.

Color C: 4 (6, 8) rows.

Color G: *K1, P1, rep from * across.

Color G: 1 (2, 3) rows.

Color A: 2 rows.

Color B: 1 row.

Color A: 1 row.

Color B: 1 row.

Color A: 1 row.

Color B: 1 row.

Color A: 2 rows.

Color E: 3 (6, 9) rows.

Color F: 2 (3, 4) rows.

Color C: *Work 1 st, sl 1 (color F), rep from * across.

Color C: 3 (5, 7) rows.

Change to color A. On next row dec 14 (16, 16) sts evenly across row. Work in K1, P1 ribbing until sleeve measures 10 (12, 14)". BO cuff.

NECK EDGING

With RS facing and color A, PU 80 (84, 96) sts around neck opening, including those sts on st holders. Place marker to designate beg of rnd, and join ends. Knit 6 rnds. BO loosely, letting neck edge roll over.

FINISHING

Sew sleeve seams together. With color E, single crochet around hem of sweater. Block garment lightly. Fold cuff over if desired.

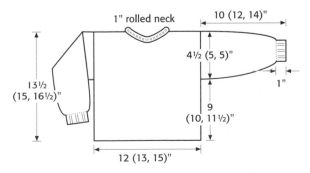

Socks

This pattern is sized Medium.

•

FINISHED MEASUREMENTS

Toe to Heel: 7"
Cuff to Heel: 5½"
Foot Circumference: 7"

MATERIALS

- Patons Grace, 50-gram skeins (136 yds), 100% cotton. In some cases, the remnant yarn from the pullover will be sufficient to make the socks. If these socks are being worked independently, use 1 skein of each of the foll colors:

  Color A: 60040 Night (black)
  Color B: 60005 Snow (white)
  Color C: 60438 Fuchsia
  Color D: 60712 Lime
  Color E: 60625 Sungold
  Color F: 60134 Royal
  Color G: 60724 Teal

- Size 4 double-pointed needles (1 set)
- Size 4 circular needle (24")
- Tapestry needle

STITCH GAUGE

26 STS and 34 rows = 4" in stockinette stitch. To save time, always check your gauge. If necessary, change needle size to obtain the correct gauge. .

NOTE: *Socks are quick, fun, and easy. Don't be intimidated by how many words it takes to explain how to knit them.*

TOP

WITH SIZE 4 circular needle and color C, CO 42 sts. Transfer sts to the dpn, placing 14 sts on needle #1, 14 sts on needle #2, and 14 sts on needle #3.

> TIP: When working on dpn, as you move from one needle to the next, cross the tip of the new needle over the tip of the one just worked. Hold the yarn firmly to work the first st on the new needle.

Rnds 1–5: *K1, P1, rep from * around.
Rnds 6–17: Color D, *K1, P1, rep from * around.
Rnds 18–20: Color G, knit.
Rnds 21 and 22: Color A, knit.
Rnd 23: Color B, knit.
Rnd 24: Color A, knit.
Rnd 25: Color B, knit.
Rnds 26 and 27: Color A, knit.
Rnds 28–33: Color E, knit.
Rnds 34–37: Color F, knit.
Rnd 38: Color C, *K1, sl 1 (color F), rep from * around.
Rnds 39–43: Color C, knit.
Rnds 44–46: Color A, knit.

HEEL

TO REPOSITION sts for heel and instep: With color D, knit across 14 sts on needle #1, 14 sts on needle #2, and 7 sts on needle #3. Place 7 sts just worked from needle #3 onto needle #2. Place last st on needle #1 onto needle #2. The 22 sts on needle #2 are instep sts to be worked later. Place 7 sts rem on needle #3 and 13 sts on needle #1 onto one needle and work heel on 20 sts in back and forth rows as follows:
Row 1: (WS) Sl 1, purl to end.
Row 2: (RS) Sl 1, *K1, sl 1, rep from *, end K1.
Rep these 2 rows until heel measures ¾", ending on RS row. With color G, work rows 1 and 2 for 4 rows. Change back to color D and work 2-row rep until heel measures 1½", ending on RS row.
To turn heel, work the foll 8 rows with color D:
Row 1 (WS): P12, P2tog, P1, turn work—19 sts.
Row 2 (RS): Sl 1, K5, ssk, K1, turn work—18 sts.
Row 3: Sl 1, P6, P2tog, P1, turn—17 sts.
Row 4: Sl 1, K7, ssk, K1, turn—16 sts.
Row 5: Sl 1, P8, P2tog, P1, turn—15 sts.
Row 6: Sl 1, K9, ssk, K1, turn—14 sts.
Row 7: Sl 1, P10, P2tog, turn—13 sts.
Row 8: Sl 1, K10, ssk, 12 sts rem.

INSTEP

SLIP FIRST 6 sts worked in row 8 onto a spare needle. Cont with same needle holding 6 sts, PU 11 sts from side of heel, putting 17 sts on needle #1; return to idle instep needle and work across 22 sts for needle #2. For needle #3, PU 11 sts from other side of heel plus 6 sts that had been placed on a spare needle. Work 56 sts on 3 needles in the rnd to shape instep as follows:
Rnd 1: Color E, knit.
Rnd 2: Color E, on needle #1, knit to last 3 sts, ssk, K1; on needle #2, knit all sts; on needle #3, K2tog, knit rem sts.

Rep rnds 1 and 2 until 5 rnds of color E have been completed. Cont working rnds 1 and 2, changing color in the foll sequence:

Color G: 6 rnds.

Color A: 1 rnd.

Color F: 3 rnds.

When needles #1 and #3 each have 10 sts rem, discontinue dec. Work across 10 sts on needle #1, work 1 st on needle #2 and place it on needle #1, work 21 sts on needle #2 and place last st on needle #3, work rem 10 sts on needle #3. There are now 11 sts on needle #1, 20 sts on needle #2, and 11 sts on needle #3. Cont in color patt as follows:

Color C: *K2, sl 2, rep from * for 1 rnd.

Color F: 3 rnds.

Color A: 1 rnd.

Color E: 3 rnds.

Color D: 1 rnd.

Color D: *K1, P1, rep from * for 1 rnd.

Color C: 6 rnds.

Color A: 2 rnds.

When foot measures approx 4¾" from heel, beg toe shaping. (Measure your child's foot. A few rows shorter or longer will not alter the outcome of these socks. You may want to add a few rows in a color of your choice for extra growth room or subtract a few rows for tiny feet.) For last rnds, work 1 rnd in color B, 2 rnds in color A, 8 rnds in color D, and color G to end. At the same time, finish toe shaping as follows:

Rnd 1: On needle #1, knit to last 3 sts, ssk, K1; on needle #2, K1, K2tog, knit to last 3 sts, ssk, K1; on needle #3, K1, K2tog, knit rem sts.

Rnd 2: Knit.

Rep these 2 rnds until 5 sts rem on needle #1, 10 sts on needle #2, and 5 sts on needle #3. You will discontinue dec on needle #2 one rnd early. Cont dec on needles #1 and #3 until the stated amount of sts rem. Combine sts on needles #1 and #3 so that you have 2 needles with 10 sts each. Cut yarn, leaving a tail approx 30" long.

Weave toe sts as follows:

Step 1: With WS facing together, holding both needles tog and even, insert tapestry needle into first st on front needle purlwise and pull yarn through. Leave st on needle.

Step 2: Holding yarn in back, insert needle knitwise into first st on back needle and pull yarn through. Leave st on needle.

Step 3: With yarn in front, insert needle knitwise through first st of front needle again and sl st off needle. Insert needle through next st on front needle purlwise and pull through. Leave st on needle.

Step 4: Insert needle purlwise through first st on back needle and slip off needle. Insert needle knitwise through next st on back needle and pull yarn through. Leave this st on needle.

Rep steps 3 and 4 until all but 1 st has been eliminated. Pull yarn through to secure.

Step 3: Insert needle knitwise through first stitch on front needle.

Insert needle purlwise through next stitch on front needle.

Step 4: Insert needle purlwise through first stitch on back needle.

Insert needle knitwise through next stitch on back needle.

This weaving technique leaves a firm but flat seam, which lends itself to the toe of a sock. It does take concentration due to the fact that you are passing yarn through a st twice, once purlwise and once knitwise, before slipping it off the needle.

Tri-Color Tweed Pullover

$\mathcal{T}$weeds are timeless, and this one is sure to be a crowd pleaser for a long while. The pullover is designed to look striking on either a girl or a boy. Work this one up in any three colors you like. The best part is that it only *looks* complicated!

MATERIALS

- Tahki Cotton Classic, 50-gram skeins (108 yds), 100% cotton

  Color A: 3764 Green   2 (3, 3, 4) skeins
  Color B: 3808 Aqua   2 (2, 3, 4) skeins
  Color C: 3873 Royal   2 (2, 3, 4) skeins

- Size 6 circular needle (24")
- Stitch holders
- Yarn needle

GAUGE

22 STITCHES and 28 rows = 4" in pattern stitch. To save time, always check your gauge. If necessary, change needle size to obtain correct gauge.

BODY

THIS SWEATER is not knit in the round, but we recommend using a circular needle and working the garment in one piece to the armholes. With color A, CO 145 (153, 157, 165) sts.

Rows 1–10: *K1, P1, rep from * across.

Row 11: Purl.

Beg 3-color basketweave sl st patt.

Multiple of 4 sts plus 1

Row 1 (RS): Color B, K1, *K3, sl 1 wyib; rep from *, end K4.

Row 2: Color B, K1, * K3, sl 1 wyif; rep from *, end K4.

Row 3: Color A, K2, * sl 1 wyib, K3; rep from *, end sl 1, K2.

Row 4: Color A, P2, * sl 1 wyif, P3; rep from *, end sl 1, P2.

Rows 5 and 6: Color C, rep rows 1 and 2.

Rows 7 and 8: Color A, rep rows 3 and 4.

Rep rows 1–8.

Cont in slip st patt until garment measures 8 (8½, 9, 10½)"; then divide into 72 (76, 78, 82) sts for front and 73 (77, 79, 83) sts for back. Place back sts on st holder. Work front sts in color sequence (adjust as needed to maintain color patt) until front measures 10 (11, 11½, 13)". Beg front neck and shoulder shaping.

FRONT NECK AND SHOULDER SHAPING

WORK IN patt across 23 (24, 25, 26) sts and place ctr 26 (28, 28, 30) sts on st holder. Join yarn and work in patt across rem 23 (24, 25, 26) sts. Work both shoulders in patt, dec 1 st at neck edge every row 5 times. When front measures 12 (13, 14, 16)", BO 18 (19, 20, 21) sts for each shoulder or place on st holder for 3-needle BO.

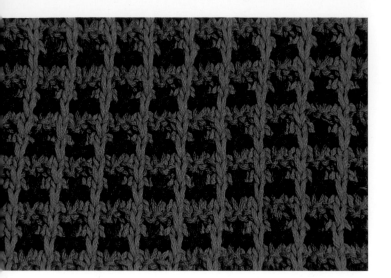

BACK

PLACE BACK sts on needle and work same as front omitting front neck shaping. When back measures 12 (13, 14, 16)", BO 18 (19, 20, 21) sts for each shoulder or place on st holder for 3-needle BO, and place ctr 37 (39, 39, 41) sts on st holder. Join front and back shoulders.

SLEEVES

Make 2.
SLEEVES ARE knit from the top down. They are not knit in the round, but we recommend using a circular needle.

Left sleeve: With RS facing and color A, PU 45 (49, 57, 61) sts evenly around opening. Work sleeve in basketweave sl st patt until sleeve measures 9 (10, 11, 13)". On next row, with color A, dec 10 (11, 12, 14) sts evenly across row. Work 5 rows of K1, P1 rib for cuff. BO.

Right sleeve: Place markers 4 (4½, 5, 5½)" from shoulder seam on front and back. With RS facing and color A, PU 45 (49, 57, 61) sts evenly between markers. Work as for left sleeve.

NECK EDGING

WITH RS facing and color A, beg at a shoulder seam and PU 80 (84, 88, 94) sts around neck opening, including sts on st holders. Place marker to designate beg of rnd, and join ends. Knit 4 rnds. BO loosely, letting neck edge roll over.

FINISHING

SEW SLEEVE seams together. Sew right side seam together. Lightly block sweater.

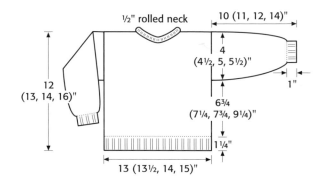

Festive Fella Pullover

𝒯his pullover is made-to-order for the energetic young fella you know. We wanted to create a vibrant pullover that used the entrelac technique, which is more often found in garments for adults. The dramatic buttons by Zecca pick up the colors in the garment and give it a special flair. It's perfect for the little guy in your life.

This pattern is sized 2T (4T, 6).

•

FINISHED MEASUREMENTS

Chest: 26½ (29, 31½)"
Length: 13 (15, 17)"
Sleeve: 10 (12, 14)"

MATERIALS

- Tahki Cotton Classic, 50-gram skeins (108 yds), 100% cotton

Color A: 3940 Purple	2 (2, 3) skeins
Color B: 3783 Aqua	5 (5, 6) skeins
Color C: 3997 Red	1 (1, 1) skein
Color D: 3533 Yellow	1 (1, 1) skein
Color E: 3401 Orange	1 (1, 1) skein

- Size 6 circular needle (24")
- Stitch holders
- Yarn needle
- 3 (4, 4) rainbow buttons, ⅝" diameter (garment buttons shown are by Zecca)

GAUGE

20 stitches and 38 rows = 4" in seed stitch. To save time, always check your gauge. If necessary, change needle size to obtain correct gauge.

BODY

This pullover is not knit in the round, but we recommend using a circular needle and working the garment in one piece to the beg of the entrelac section. With color A, CO 150 (166, 182) sts. Work 3 rows in K1, P1 rib. Cont in rib for 2 (2, 3) rows each of colors E, C, D, and B. Next row, with color A, seed st across row (see page 20). Cont in seed st until piece measures 4 (6¼, 7)". Cont in seed st for 2 rows each of colors E, C, and D. Next row, with color B, knit (RS row) or purl (WS row) across row, dec 50 (56, 62) sts evenly—100 (110, 120) sts. Divide sts for back and front. Next row, knit (RS rows) or purl (WS row) across 50 (55, 60) sts for back, and place rem 50 (55, 60) sts on st holder for front. If necessary, work one more row to end on RS row.

BACK

With WS facing and color B, beg base triangles as follows:

Step 1: *Base Triangles:* With purl side of work facing, *P2, turn garment so that RS is facing; K2, turn again so that WS is facing; P3, turn; K3, turn; P4, turn, K4; turn, P5; do not turn. These sts form 1 base triangle. Leave sts on the needle and rep from * to make a total of 10 (11, 12) triangles with 5 sts each.

Step 2: *Right Side Triangle:* With RS facing, K2, turn; P2, turn; inc 1 st in first st, sl next st from LH needle to RH needle, K1, psso; turn, P3, turn; inc 1 st in first st, K1, sl 1, K1, psso, turn; P4, turn; inc 1 st in first st, K2, sl 1, K1, psso, do not turn, end on RS row with 5 sts on needle.

Step 3: *Left-Sloping Rectangles:* With RS facing, PU and knit 5 sts down side edge of base triangle, turn; P5, turn; *K4, sl 1, K1, psso, turn; P5, turn; rep from * until all sts have been worked off left needle. Cont in this manner until all base triangles have been worked, ending on RS row; do not turn.

Step 4: *Left Side Triangle:* With RS facing, PU and knit 5 sts down edge of last base triangle, turn; P2tog, P3, turn; K4, turn; P2tog, P2, turn; K3, turn; P2tog, P1, turn; K2, turn; P2tog, place 1 rem st on LH needle.

Step 5: *Right-Sloping Rectangles:* With WS facing, P1 placed on needle and PU and purl 4 sts down edge of rectangle, turn; *K5, turn; P4, P2tog, turn; rep from * until all sts have been dec and 1 right-sloping rectangle is completed. Do not turn. PU and P5 sts down edge of each of the next rectangles. Cont as above between *s, working each group of sts off the left needle to end.

> **HINTS:** Steps 2 and 4 form triangles, and steps 3 and 5 form rectangles. Whether on a triangle or a rectangle, use the side edge for picking up sts. Right-sloping and left-sloping rectangle instructions are repeated across all groups of sts on the LH needle. Right side and left side triangles are worked only at the designated end of a group of rectangles.

Work all steps as presented one time. For sizes 2T and 4T, work steps 2–5 two times more. For size 6, work steps 2–5 three times more. For all sizes, work steps 2, 3, and 4 one time more, and then work step 6, which will finish the entrelac section of the garment.

Step 6: *Top or Closing Triangles:* (WS) With *1 st on the needle from the left side triangle, PU and P4 sts along end of side triangle, turn; K5, turn; P2tog, P1, P2tog, turn; K3, turn; P2tog, P1, turn; K2, turn; P2tog, 1 st rem, do not turn. Rep across rectangles from * until 1 st at right edge rem, fasten off.

With RS facing and color B, PU and knit 75 (83, 91) sts along top edge of closing triangles. Est seed st in next row and cont on rows until garment measures 12½ (14½, 16½)". Cont in patt across 23 (25, 27) sts for right shoulder; place 29 (33, 37) ctr sts on st holder. Join second ball of yarn and work in patt across 23 (25, 27) sts for left shoulder. Cont on each shoulder, dec 1 st at neck edge every row 2 times. When back measures 13 (15, 17)", BO 21 (23, 25) sts for each shoulder or place on st holder for 3-needle BO.

FRONT

PU sts from st holder, attach color B, and if necessary, work a row across front to match the back section. Work 2 sections of front separately. On WS row, beg entrelac patt for right front on 25 (25, 30) sts for 5 (5, 6) base triangles of 5 sts each. Place rem 25 (30, 30) sts for left front on st holder. Refer to steps 1–6 of entrelac patt and work as for back. For left front, PU sts from st holder, attach yarn at ctr front, and rep entrelac patt as for right side—with one exception. For size 4T, BO 5 sts at ctr front, and then rep patt as for right side. When right and left front sections are complete through step 6, PU 35 (39, 43) sts along BO of top triangle for 1 front section. Est seed st in next row and cont until front measures 12 (14, 15½)". Next RS row for right front, WS row for left front: BO 10 (10, 12) sts at neck edge. Cont in patt, dec 1 st at neck edge EOR 4 (6, 6) times. When front measures 13 (15, 17)", BO 21 (23, 25) sts or place on st holder for 3-needle BO. Rep for other side of front. Join shoulder seams.

SLEEVES

Make 2.

SLEEVES ARE knit from the top down. They are not knit in the round, but we recommend using a circular needle. Place markers 4½ (5½, 6)" from shoulder seam on front and back. With RS facing and color B, PU 51 (61, 67) sts evenly between markers. Est seed st and work 1 row in color B, and 2 rows each of colors D, C, E, and A. Switch to color B and cont in patt until sleeve measures 3 (4, 4)".

BUTTON BAND

ON RIGHT front edge, with RS facing and color B, PU 32 (38, 42) sts. Work in K2, P2 rib for 5 (7, 5) rows. BO in patt. Rep on left front edge, placing 3 (4, 4) buttonholes evenly spaced in row 3 (4, 3). (See "Buttonholes" on page 13.) At bottom of placket button band, stitch edge down at front ctr to secure. For size 4T, use the wider button band to span the wider opening in the ctr. Stitch the left-side band bottom down across the 5-st opening.

COLLAR

WITH RS facing and color A, beg at top ctr of right front band and PU 70 (80, 94) sts evenly around neck edge, ending at ctr of left band. Work in K1, P1 rib in foll color sequence:
Color A: 10 (12, 14) rows.
Colors B, D, C, and E: 2 rows each.
Color A: BO in patt.

FINISHING

SEW OPEN side seam together; use Purple yarn for bottom and change to Aqua for entrelac section and sleeves. Place buttons on band to correspond with buttonholes. Do not block the entrelac portion of this garment. Let it puff out.

Dec 1 st at each edge every 10 rows 2 (3, 3) times. Cont in patt to 8 (10, 12)"; dec 3 (7, 9) sts evenly in next row. For cuff, work K1, P1 rib in the foll color sequence:
Color A: 4 rows.
Colors B, D, C, and E: 2 rows each.
Color A: 1 row.
Color A: BO in patt.

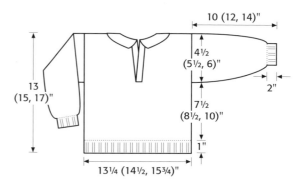

Swiss Miss Pullover with Scarf

We've always thought that a bit of entrelac was fun and special, but a lot of entrelac is a little overwhelming for a child's garment. When we combined a form-fitting slip-stitch pattern with the high texture of entrelac, we ended up with a very stylized, tunic-length pullover that reminded us of some old European designs of years ago. The additional intarsia motifs are charming, and your favorite tot will also be charming in this outfit.

Pullover

This pattern is sized 2T (4T, 6).

●

FINISHED MEASUREMENTS

Chest: 24 (28, 32)"
Length: 13½ (16, 17½)"
Three-Quarter-Length Sleeve: 8 (9½, 11)"
Bottom Circumference: 31 (33, 37)"

MATERIALS

- Tahki Cotton Classic, 50-gram skeins (108 yds), 100% cotton

Color A: 3997 Red	6 (7, 9) skeins
Color B: 3923 Lavender	1 (1, 2) skeins
Color C: 3764 Green	1 (1, 2) skeins
Color D: 3533 Yellow	1 (1, 2) skeins

- Size 6 circular needle (24")
- Size 5 circular needle (24")
- Stitch holders
- Yarn needle

GAUGE

21 STITCHES and 36 rows = 4" in striped slip-stitch pattern on size 6 needles.

15 stitches and 32 rows = approx 4" in entrelac stitch pattern on size 6 needles.

To save time, always check your gauge. If necessary, change needle size to obtain correct gauge.

NOTE: *This pullover as shown has three graphed designs (page 41) worked into the left-sloping rectangles of the entrelac patt. You can choose to use the same designs or select other motifs, and you can also place them in the pullover where you want. Or you may decide that you want to leave them out entirely. Directions indicate when you have reached the set of rectangles to decorate. The graphs are specific as to placement.*

FRONT

THIS PULLOVER is not knit in the round, but we recommend using a circular needle. With size 6 needle and color B, CO 60 (64, 72) sts. Work bottom edging.

Row 1 (WS): P1, *P2 tog, YO, rep from *, end P1.

Row 2 (RS): K2, *K2 tog, YO, rep from *, end K2.

Beg entrelac patt for pullover body of 6 (7, 8) base triangles of 10 (9, 9) sts each as follows:

Step 1: *Base Triangles:* With WS facing, *P2, turn garment so that RS is facing; K2, turn again so WS is facing; P3, turn; K3, turn; P4, turn; K4, turn; P5, turn; K5, turn; P6, turn; K6, turn; P7, turn; K7, turn; P8, turn; K8, turn; P9; do not turn (size 2T does turn; K9, turn; P10; do not turn). These sts form 1 base triangle. Leave sts on the needle and rep from * to make a total of 6 (7, 8) triangles with 10 (9, 9) sts each.

Step 2: *Right Side Triangle:* With RS of work facing, K2, turn; P2, turn; inc 1 st in first st, sl next st on LH needle to RH needle, K1, psso, turn; P3, turn; inc 1 st in first st, K1, sl 1, K1, psso, turn; P4, turn; inc 1 st in first st, K2, sl 1, K1, turn. Cont in this manner until 10 (9, 9) sts are on needle, ending on RS row; do not turn.

Step 3: *Left-Sloping Rectangle* (Graphed designs can be worked into this set of rectangles): With RS facing, PU and knit 10 (9, 9) sts down side edge of base triangle, turn; P10 (9, 9), turn; *K9 (8, 8), sl 1, K1, psso, turn; P10 (9, 9), turn; rep from * until all sts have been worked off left needle, ending on RS row. Cont in this manner until 5 (6, 7) base triangles have been worked, ending on RS row; do not turn.

Step 4: *Left Side Triangle:* With RS facing, PU and knit 10 (9, 9) sts down edge of last base triangle, turn; P2tog, P8 (7, 7), turn; K9 (8, 8), turn; P2tog, P7 (6, 6), turn; K8 (7, 7), turn; P2tog, P6 (5, 5), turn; K7 (6, 6), turn. Cont in patt until P2tog leaves 1 st rem on needle. Do not turn. Move 1 st to LH needle.

Step 5: *Right-Sloping Rectangles:* With WS facing, P1 st from left side triangle that was placed on needle and PU and purl 9 (8, 8) st down edge of rectangle, turn; *K10 (9, 9), turn; P9 (8, 8), P2tog, turn; rep from * until all sts have been dec and 1 right-sloping rectangle is completed. With WS facing, PU and purl 10 (9, 9) down edge of each of the next rectangles. Rep between *s, working each group of sts off the left needle to end.

Work steps 2–5 as presented one time. For size 2T, cont on steps 2–5 one time more. For sizes 4T–6, work steps 2–5 two times more. For all sizes, work steps 2, 3, and 4 one time more, and then work step 6, which will finish the entrelac section of the garment.

HINTS: Steps 2 and 4 form triangles, and steps 3 and 5 form rectangles. Whether on a triangle or a rectangle, use the side edge for picking up sts. Right-sloping and left-sloping rectangle instructions are repeated across all groups of sts on the LH needle. Right side and left side triangles are worked only at the designated end of a group of rectangles.

Step 6: *Top or Closing Triangles:* With WS facing and *with 1 st on the needle from the left side triangle, PU and purl 9 (8, 8) sts along end of side triangle, turn; K10 (9, 9), turn; P2tog, P6 (5, 5), P2tog, turn; K8 (7, 7), turn; P2tog, P4 (3, 3), P2tog, turn; K6 (5, 5), turn; P2tog, P2, P2tog, turn; K4 (3, 3), turn; P2tog, P2tog for 2T (P1, P2tog for sizes 4T and 6), turn; P2tog, 1 st rem, do not turn. Rep across all rectangles from * until 1 st at right edge rem. Fasten off.

With RS facing and color A, switch to size 5 needle and PU and knit 67 (79, 91) sts along top edge of closing triangles. Next row: With color B, purl. Switch to size 6 needle, work striped sl st patt as follows:

Row 1 (RS): Color A, K1, * sl 1 wyib, K3; rep from *, end sl 1, K1.

Row 2 (WS): Color A, P1, *sl 1 wyif, P3, rep from *, end sl 1, P1.

Row 3: Color D, * K3, sl 1 wyib, rep from *, end K3.

Row 4: Color D, * P3, sl 1 wyif, rep from *, end P3.

Rows 5 and 6: Color C, rep rows 1 and 2.

Rows 7 and 8: Color B, rep rows 3 and 4.

Rep this 8-row patt until front measures 12 (14, 15)".

FRONT NECK AND SHOULDER SHAPING

WORK IN patt across 22 (26, 31) sts, and place 23 (27, 29) ctr sts on st holder for neck. Join yarn and work in patt across rem 22 (26, 31) sts. Work both shoulders, dec 1 st at neck edge EOR 3 times. Cont working shoulder sts until garment measures 13½" (16, 17½)". Place 19 (23, 28) sts for each shoulder on st holder for 3-needle BO.

BACK

WORK AS for front, cont 8-row patt until back measures 13 (15½, 17)". Next row: Work across 21 (25, 30) sts, and place 25 (29, 31) ctr sts on st holder. Join second ball of yarn and work across rem 21 (25, 30) sts. Work both shoulders, dec 1 st at neck edge every row 2 times. Cont working shoulder sts as for front. Place 19 (23, 28) sts for each shoulder on st holder for 3-needle BO. Join front and back shoulders.

THREE-QUARTER-LENGTH SLEEVES

SLEEVES ARE worked from the top down. They are not knit in the round, but we recommend using a circular needle. Place markers 4 (4½, 5)" from shoulder seam on front and back. With size 5 needle, RS facing, and color A, PU 51 (59, 67) sts evenly spaced between markers. Work in St st until sleeve measures 6 (7½, 9)". Work 16 rows of striped sl st in the foll color sequence:

Rows 1–2: Color B.
Rows 3–4: Color C.
Rows 5–6: Color D.
Rows 7–8: Color A.

Rep rows 1–8 one time. Next row, knit 1 row in color B. BO in color B.

NECK EDGING

WITH SIZE 6 needle, RS facing, and color A, beg at shoulder seam and PU 70 (80, 94) sts around neck edge, including sts on st holders. Neck sts are not worked in the round. Work 4 rows in K2, P2 rib. Switch to color B and work one more row in est rib. BO in purl st on RS.

FINISHING

SEW SLEEVE seams and side seams together. Sew neck ribbing at shoulder seam.

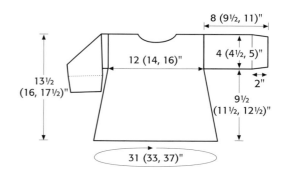

GRAPHS

THE ENTRELAC technique forms rectangular blocks that are prime canvases for creative designs. The intarsia motifs are worked in St st on left-sloping (LS) rectangles only. Cut lengths of yarn approx 12" to 16" for each color used in the graphs. Proceed in the foll manner from right to left across each set of rectangles.

For 2T

First set of 5 LS rectangles: (1) graph 1, (2) blank, (3) graph 2, (4) blank, (5) graph 1.

Second set of 5 LS rectangles: (1) graph 3, (2) graph 2, (3) blank, (4) graph 2, (5) graph 3. Rep instructions for first set.

For 4T

First set of 6 LS rectangles: (1) graph 1, (2) blank, (3) graph 2, (4) graph 2, (5) blank, (6) graph 1.

Second set of 6 LS rectangles: (1) blank, (2) graph 3, (3) blank, (4) blank, (5) graph 3, (6) blank. Rep first and second set of LS rectangles.

For Size 6

First set of 7 LS rectangles: (1) graph 1, (2) blank, (3) graph 2, (4) blank, (5) graph 2, (6) blank, (7) graph 1.

Second set of 7 LS rectangles: (1) blank, (2) graph 2, (3) blank, (4) graph 3, (5) blank, (6) graph 2, (7) blank. Rep first and second set of LS rectangles.

Swiss Miss, Graph 1

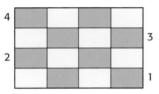

Work 4 st x 4 row design in St st.
Beg graph 1 in row 7 of a left-sloping
rectangle. Work 3 sts, work 4-st graph,
and work 3 (2, 2) sts.

Swiss Miss, Graph 3

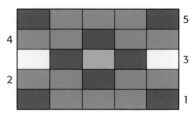

Work 5 st x 5 row design in St st.
Beg graph 3 in row 7 of a left-sloping
rectangle. Work 2 sts, work 5-st graph,
and work 3 (2, 2) sts.

Swiss Miss, Graph 2

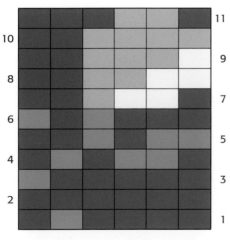

Work 6 st x 11 row design in St st.
Beg graph 2 in row 5 of a left-sloping
rectangle. Work 2 sts, work 6-st graph,
and work 2 (1, 1) sts.

Scarf

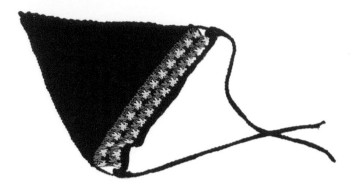

DIRECTIONS

WITH SIZE 5 needle and color A, CO 59 (67) sts.

Rows 1 and 2: Knit.

Next 16 (20) rows: Striped sl st patt (see "Swiss Miss Pullover" on page 38).

Next row (RS): Color A, ssk, knit to last 2 sts, K2tog.

Next row: Purl.

Cont in St st, dec 1 st on each side of RS rows to last st. Pull yarn through to secure.

With medium-sized crochet hook, chain 10 sts to make loop for tie, leaving tails at both ends. Pull 1 tail through the beg of the CO row for the scarf, and other tail through the edge of the sl st. Tie tails off on WS and secure ends; this forms a loop. Rep on other side. Make 2 more chains approx 12 (13)" long. Pull through loops attached to scarf and tie off.

This pattern is sized Small/Medium (Large).

•

FINISHED MEASUREMENTS

Head Band: 9 (10½)"

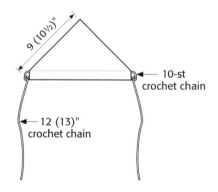

9 (10½)"

10-st crochet chain

12 (13)" crochet chain

MATERIALS

- Tahki Cotton Classic, 50-gram skein (108 yds), 100% cotton. In some cases, the remnant yarn from the pullover will be sufficient to make a head scarf. If this scarf is being done independently, use 1 skein of each of the foll colors:

  Color A: 3997 Red
  Color B: 3923 Lavender
  Color C: 3764 Green
  Color D: 3533 Yellow

- Size 5 circular needle (24")
- Medium-sized crochet hook

GAUGE

23 STITCHES and 32 rows = 4" in stockinette stitch.

Classy Cables Pullover with Hat

$\mathcal{W}$e love this design just as it is. It is classic in color, style, and simplicity. The yarn has a little wool in it to give the pullover weight and warmth without bulk. We see endless possibilities for working it in color, color block, or stripes. Because it is a unisex design, we will be surprised if we don't see many of you doing it your way for both Jimmy and Jane.

Pullover

This pattern is sized 2T (4T, 6, 8).

•

FINISHED MEASUREMENTS

Chest Width: 25 (28, 31, 34)"
Length: 13 (14½, 16, 17½)"
Sleeve Length: 10 (12, 14, 15)"

MATERIALS

- 5 (6, 8, 10) skeins Cotton Connection D.K. No. 2 by Naturally, 50-gram skein (108 yds), 84% cotton, 10% wool, 6% nylon; color #02
- Size 6 circular needle (24")
- Size 7 circular needle (24") for neck BO
- Cable needle
- Stitch holders
- Yarn needle
- Buttons, ¾" diameter (optional)
- For bear pullover, see page 47.

GAUGE

22 STITCHES and 32 rows = 4" in pattern stitch. To save time, always check your gauge. If necessary, change needle size to obtain correct gauge.

STITCH PATTERNS

Broken Rib
Row 1: K1, P1.
Row 2: Purl.
Rep rows 1 and 2.

16-Row Diamond Cable (10-st cable) for Pullover Body
Work on 23 ctr sts.
Row 1 (RS): K6, sl 2 sts to cable needle (cn) and hold in back, K2, K2 from cn.
Row 2 and all WS rows: Purl.
Row 3: K4, sl 2 sts to cn, hold in back, K2, K2 from cn; K2.
Row 5: K2, sl 2 sts to cn, hold in back, K2, K2 from cn; K4.
Row 7: Sl 2 sts to cn, hold in back, K2, K2 from cn; K6.
Row 9: Sl 2 sts to cn, hold in front, K2, K2 from cn; K6.
Row 11: K2, sl 2 sts to cn, hold in front, K2, K2 from cn; K4.
Row 13: K4, sl 2 sts to cn, hold in front, K2, K2 from cn; K2.
Row 15: K6, sl 2 sts to cn, hold in front, K2, K2 from cn.
Row 16: Purl.
For left side cable, beg with row 9, work through row 16, and then work rows 1–8.
For right side cable, beg with row 1, work through row 16.

12-Row Diamond Cable (8-st cable) for Sleeves
Work on 19 ctr sts.
Row 1: K4, sl 2 sts to cn and hold in back, K2, now K2 from cn.
Row 2 and all WS rows: Purl all sts.

Row 3: K2, sl 2 sts to cn and hold in back, K2, now K2 from cn; K2.

Row 5: Sl 2 sts to cn and hold in back, K2, now K2 from cn; K4.

Row 7. Sl 2 sts to cn and hold in front, K2, now K2 from cn; K4.

Row 9: K2, sl 2 sts to cn and hold in front, K2, now K2 from cn; K2.

Row 11: K4, sl 2 sts to cn and hold in front, K2, now K2 from cn.

Row 12: Purl.

For left side cable, beg with row 7, work through row 12, and then work rows 1–6.

For right side cable, beg with row 1 and work through row 12.

FRONT

THIS PULLOVER is not knit in the round, but we recommend using a circular needle. With size 6 needle, CO 71 (79, 87, 95) sts. Work 3 (3, 5, 5) rows in garter st (knit every row) for bottom rib. Beg broken rib patt and 16-row diamond cable patt:

Row 1 (RS): Work broken rib patt, K1, P1 across 24 (28, 32, 36) sts for left side, place marker, work 10 sts in 16-row cable patt beg with row 9 (left side cable), 3 sts in P1, K1, P1 (ctr sts), 10 sts in 16-row cable patt beg with row 1 (right side cable), place marker, work broken rib patt, P1, K1, across rem 24 (28, 32, 36) sts for right side section.

Row 2: Purl.

Rep rows 1 and 2, working in patt as est until front measures 13 (14½, 16, 17½)", ending on WS row. Beg front neck and shoulder shaping.

FRONT NECK AND SHOULDER SHAPING

PLACE 18 (20, 22, 24) sts on st holder, join yarn, and cont in patt across 35 (39, 43, 47) ctr sts. Place rem 18 (20, 22, 24) sts on st holder. For T-neck shaping, cont in patt for 3 (5, 5, 7) rows. Next WS row, knit. Next RS row, switch to size 7 needle and purl all sts. For sizes 6 and 8: Work 2 rows of WS knit and RS purl. BO loosely in knit st.

BACK

WITH SIZE 6 needles, CO 71 (79, 87, 95) sts. Work bottom rib in 3 (3, 5, 5) rows of garter st as for front. Beg broken rib patt:

Row 1 (RS): K1, P1 across row.

Row 2: Purl.

Rep rows 1 and 2 until back measures 13 (14½, 16, 17½)", ending on WS row. Place 18 (20, 22, 24) sts on st holder, join yarn, and cont in patt across 35 (39, 43, 47) ctr sts, place rem 18 (20, 22, 24) sts on st holder. Work T-neck as for front. Join shoulders with 3-needle BO.

SLEEVES

Make 2.

Sleeves are worked from the top down. They are not knit in the round, but we recommend using a circular needle. Place markers 4½ (5, 5½, 5½)" from shoulder seam on front and back. With RS facing, PU 51 (55, 63, 63) sts evenly between markers. Purl next row. Beg broken rib patt and 12-row cable patt.

Row 1 (RS): K1, P1 across 16 (l8, 22, 22) sts for left side section, place marker, work 8 sts in 12-row cable patt beg with row 7 (left side cable), 3 sts in P1, K1, P1, 8 sts in 12-row cable patt beg with row 1 (right side cable), place marker, P1, K1 across rem 16 (18, 22, 22) sts for right side section.

Row 2: Purl.

Rep rows 1 and 2, staying in est patt until sleeve measures 9½ (11½, 13½, 14½)" and ends on RS row. Next WS row, knit across, dec 9 (9, 13, 13) sts evenly in row. Next RS row, purl. Next WS row, knit. Next RS row, purl. BO sts loosely.

FINISHING

Sᴇᴡ ꜱɪᴅᴇ seams and sleeve seams together. Sew each side of neck together where it extends above shoulder seam. Garment as shown has buttons sewn down front between opposing cables.

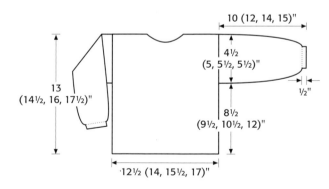

Hat

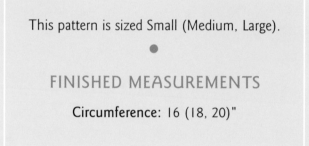

This pattern is sized Small (Medium, Large).

•

FINISHED MEASUREMENTS

Circumference: 16 (18, 20)"

MATERIALS

- 2 (2, 2) skeins Cotton Connection D.K. No. 2 by Naturally, 50-gram skein (108 yds), 84% cotton, 10% wool, 6% nylon, color #02
- Size 6 circular needle (24")
- Cable needle
- Tapestry needle

GAUGE

22 ꜱᴛɪᴛᴄʜᴇꜱ and 32 rows = 4" in pattern stitch.

BAND

WITH SIZE 6 needle, CO 16 sts. Purl next row. Beg 16-row diamond cable patt.

Row 1 (RS): K2, P1, work row 1 of 10-st cable patt, P1, K2.

Row 2: Purl.

Row 3: K2, P1, work row 3 of cable patt, P1, K2.

Row 4: Purl.

Cont in patt of K2, P1; work 10-st cable row; P1, K2 for 16 rows. Work in this 16 st and 16 row patt as for right side of pullover front a total of 7 (8, 9) times. BO sts. Lightly steam-block hat band.

BODY

PU 91 (101, 111) sts across the horizontal edge of hat band. Next row, purl. Work broken rib st as for pullover until total length of cap measures 6½ (7, 8)", ending on WS row.

CROWN

Rows 1, 3, and 5 (RS): P2tog across row.

Rows 2, 4, and 6 (WS): Knit.

Rep rows 1 and 2 one time more for size Large.

FINISHING

CUT YARN, leaving long tail to pull through rem sts. Draw up tightly to secure crown. Use rem yarn tail to join back seam.

Tassel

Make tassel by wrapping yarn 50 times around a 3" index card (a checkbook also works well). Cut a length of yarn and slip through wrapped yarn. Tie tightly and slip tassel off card. Holding tassel

16 (18, 20)"

securely by one end, cut loops at opposite end. Hold by tied end and approx ½" from tied end, tie another length of yarn tightly around the tassel. Trim tassel to approx 2¼" to 2½" long. Rep for second tassel. Lay hat flat from front to back as it will be worn. Secure tassels side by side through top ctr. Tie off on WS of cap.

BEAR PULLOVER

THE BEAR VERSION of "Classy Cables Pullover" is shown in 2T size in a color block design. Use yarn with a matching stitch gauge in the fiber content and colors of your choice.

As shown:
 Ribbing—gold
 Front—red
 Back—green
 Right sleeve—gold
 Left sleeve—green
 Sleeve edging—red

- All measurements and instructions remain the same.
- Yarn amounts are equally divided between the 3 colors. Yarn amounts as given assume 108 yards per skein.

American Spirit Pullover

Feeling patriotic? Show off the much-loved youngster in your life in red, white, and blue! The little Paul Revere will love the easy fit and comfort of this eye-catching pullover. We designed this one with even older patriots in mind. Check out the size range available.

This pattern is sized 2T (3T, 4T, 6, 8, 10).

•

FINISHED MEASUREMENTS

Chest: 24 (26½, 28½, 31, 33, 35½)"
Length: 12 (13, 14, 15, 16, 17)"
Drop Sleeve: 9 (10, 11, 12, 14, 15)"

MATERIALS

- Cascade Yarns 220, 100-gram skeins
  (220 yds), 100% wool
  Color A: 2404 Blue   1 (1, 2, 2, 2, 3) skeins
  Color B: 9404 Red   1(1, 2, 2, 2, 3) skeins
  Color C: 8505 White   1 (1, 1, 1, 1, 2) skeins
- Size 8 circular needle (24")
- Stitch holders
- Tapestry needle
- 1 star button, 1" diameter (garment button
  shown is by Mill Hill)

GAUGE

18 STITCHES and 24 rows = 4" in stockinette stitch. To save time, always check your gauge. If necessary, change needle size to obtain correct gauge.

BODY

FOR A nicer finish, the hem of this pullover is knit in the round. With color A, CO 110 (120, 130, 140, 150, 160) sts. Rnds 1–4: Knit. Rnds 5–9: Work K2, P2 rib. Divide sts for back and front. Place back 56 (60, 66, 70, 76, 80) sts on st holder. Work back and forth on front 54 (60, 64, 70, 74, 80) sts in St st until front measures 5 (5, 5, 6, 7, 7)". Cont in St st across 12 (15, 17, 20, 22, 25) sts, work flag design on ctr 30 sts (see graph on page 50), and work across rem 12 (15, 17, 20, 22, 25) sts. When flag design is complete, cont in St st for 6 rows. Change to color B, work 1 row of K1, P1 across. Work in St st until sweater front measures 10½ (11½, 12, 13, 14, 14½)". Beg front neck and shoulder shaping.

FRONT NECK AND SHOULDER SHAPING

WITH RS facing, work across 17 (19, 20, 22, 23, 25) sts. Place ctr 20 (22, 24, 26, 28, 30) sts on st holder. Join second ball of yarn and work rem 17 (19, 20, 22, 23, 25) sts. Work both shoulders in St st, dec 1 st at neck edge every row 3 times until front measures 12 (13, 14, 15, 16, 17)". BO 14 (16, 17, 19, 20, 22) sts for each shoulder or place on st holder for 3-needle BO.

BACK

PU STS from st holder and work same as front, omitting flag design and front neck shaping until garment measures 12 (13, 14, 15, 16, 17)". BO 14 (16, 17, 19, 20, 22) sts for each shoulder or place on st holder for 3-needle BO, and place ctr 28 (28, 32, 32, 36, 36) sts on holder. Join front and back shoulders.

cuff with 5 rows of K2, P2 ribbing and 4 rows of St st. BO loosely, letting cuff roll back slightly.

NECK EDGING

WITH RS facing and color B, PU 60 (62, 70, 76, 80, 86) sts around neck opening including those sts on st holders. Place marker to designate beg of rnd and join ends. Work in K2, P2 rib for 5 rnds; then knit 4 rnds. BO loosely, letting neck edge roll over.

SLEEVES

Make 2.

Sleeves are knit from the top down. They are not knit in the round, but we recommend using a circular needle. Place markers 4½ (5, 5½, 5½, 6, 6)" from shoulder seam on front and back. With RS facing and color C, PU 42 (45, 50, 50, 55, 55) sts evenly between markers. Work in St st in a 7-row stripe patt of colors C and B until sleeve measures 8 (9, 10, 11, 13, 14)". On the last row of color stripe, dec 12 (14, 16, 16, 18, 18) sts evenly across row. Working the next color in the stripe patt, create a

FINISHING

SEW SLEEVE and side seams together. Block garment lightly. Secure star button to the flag. With color C and a tapestry needle, use a running st to outline the blue section of the flag.

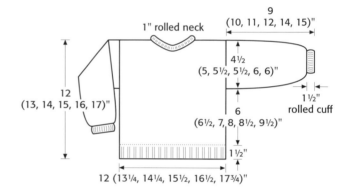

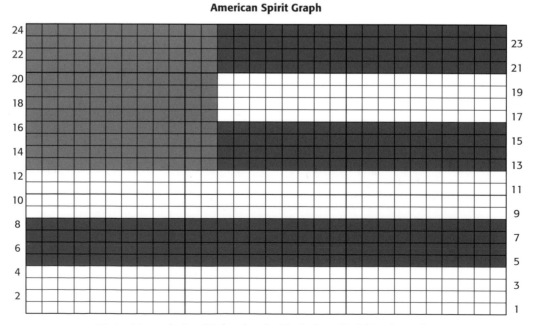

American Spirit Graph

30 st x 24 row design. Work red and white in St st. Work blue in seed st.

Salty Dog Pullover

*A*ll hands on deck! Any young mate will be seaworthy wearing this nautical number, which coordinates with "American Spirit Pullover." It makes a classic look for the next set of siblings on your knit list.

This pattern is sized 2T (3T, 4T, 6, 8, 10).

•

FINISHED MEASUREMENTS

Chest: 24 (26 ½, 28 ½, 31, 33, 35 ½)"
Length: 12 (13, 14, 15, 16, 17)"
Drop Sleeve: 9 (10, 11, 12, 14, 15)"

MATERIALS

- Cascade Yarns 220, 100-gram skeins (220 yds), 100% wool

  Color A: 2404 Blue   1 (1, 1, 1, 2, 2) skeins
  Color B: 9404 Red   1 (1, 1, 1, 2, 2) skeins
  Color C: 8505 White   1 (2, 2, 2, 2, 3) skeins

- Size 8 circular needle (24")
- Stitch holders
- Yarn needle

GAUGE

18 STITCHES and 24 rows = 4" in stockinette stitch. To save time, always check your gauge. If necessary, change needle size to obtain correct gauge.

BODY

FOR A nicer finish, the hem of this pullover is knit in the round. With color C, CO 110 (120, 130, 140, 150, 160) sts. Knit first 4 rounds. Rnd 5: Beg K2, P2 rib. Work 5 rnds of ribbing. Divide sts into front and back. Place back 55 (61, 65, 71, 75, 81) sts on st holder. Work on front 55 (59, 65, 69, 75, 79) sts in St st until front measures 2 (2, 2½, 3, 3, 3½)". Cont in St st, work across 16 (18, 21, 23, 26, 28) sts, work anchor design on next 23 sts (see graph on page 53), and work across rem 16 (18, 21, 23, 26, 28) sts. When anchor design is complete, cont in St st for 1½ (2, 2½, 3, 3, 3½)". Change to color A, work 1 row of K1, P1 across. Cont in St st until sweater front measures 10½ (11½, 12, 13, 14, 14½)". Beg front neck and shoulder shaping.

FRONT NECK AND SHOULDER SHAPING

WITH RS facing, work across 17 (19, 20, 22, 23, 25) sts. Place ctr 21 (21, 25, 25, 29, 29) sts on st holder. Join second ball of yarn and work rem 17 (19, 20, 22, 23, 25) sts. Work both shoulders in St st, dec 1 st at neck edge every row 3 times until front measures 12 (13, 14, 15, 16, 17)". BO 14 (16, 17, 19, 20, 22) sts for each shoulder or place on st holder for 3-needle BO.

BACK

PU sts from st holder and work in St st in a 7-row stripe patt of colors B and C until garment measures the same length as front section of color C. Switch to color A, work 1 row of K1, P1 across. Cont in St st until back measures 12 (13, 14, 15, 16, 17)". BO 14 (16, 17, 19, 20, 22) sts for each shoulder or place on st holder for 3-needle BO, and place ctr 27 (29, 31, 33, 35, 37) sts on holder. Join front and back shoulders.

SLEEVES

Make 2.

Sleeves are knit from the top down. They are not knit in the round, but we recommend using a circular needle. Place markers 4½ (5, 5½, 5½, 6, 6)" from shoulder seam on front and back. With RS facing and color C, PU 42 (45, 50, 50, 55, 55) sts evenly between markers. Work in St st in a 7-row stripe patt of colors C and B until sleeve measures 8 (9, 10, 11, 13, 14)". On the last row of the color stripe, dec 12 (14, 16, 16, 18, 18) sts evenly across row. With next color in stripe patt, work 5 rows of K2, P2 rib and 4 rows of St st to make cuff. BO loosely, letting cuff roll back slightly.

NECK EDGING

WITH RS facing and color A, PU 60 (62, 70, 76, 80, 86) sts around neck opening, including those sts on st holders. Place marker to designate beg of round and join ends. Work in K2, P2 rib for 24 rnds to create turtleneck. BO loosely. Fold neck over.

FINISHING

SEW SLEEVE and side seams together. Block garment lightly. With color A, crochet a chain approx 6" to 8" long. With yarn needle, secure the ends of the anchor chain, referring to photo below left. Secure middle of chain as necessary.

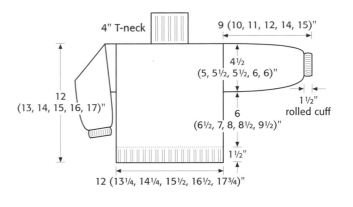

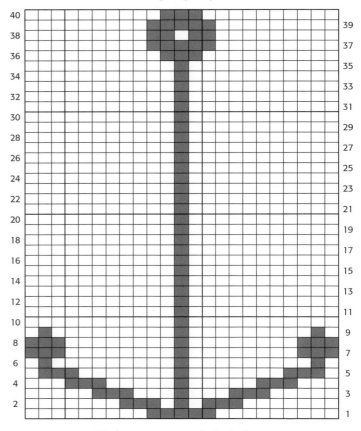

Salty Dog Graph

Work 23 st x 40 row design in St st.

Bowl of Cherries Pullover with Backpack

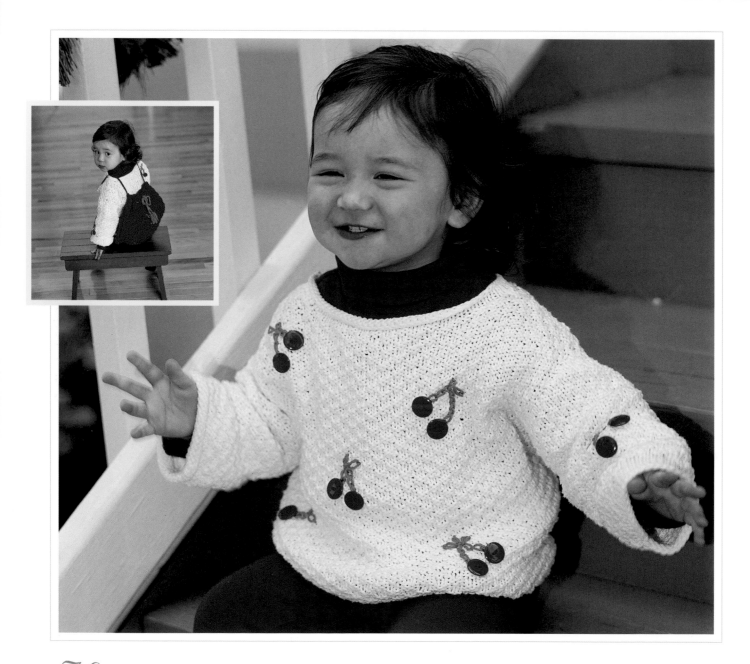

$\mathcal{H}$ave you heard the saying, "Life is just a bowl of cherries"? This little cotton pullover is just that. It's guaranteed to be a hit with the sweetheart who receives it, and she'll be happy not only to wear the pullover but also to use the matching backpack!

Pullover

This pattern is sized 2T (4T, 6).

●

FINISHED MEASUREMENTS

Chest: 26 (27½, 28¼, 30½)"
Length: 12 (13, 14, 15)"
Drop Sleeve: 10 (11, 12, 14)"

MATERIALS

- Tahki Cotton Classic, 50-gram skeins (108 yds), 100% cotton

  Color A: 3001 White   4 (5, 6, 7) skeins
  Color B: 3997 Red   a small amount
  Color C: 3764 Green   a small amount

- Size 6 circular needle (24")
- Stitch holders
- Tapestry needle
- 13 red buttons, ¾" diameter (garment buttons shown are by LaMode)

GAUGE

22 STITCHES and 28 rows = 4" in pattern stitch. To save time, always check your gauge. If necessary, change needle size to obtain correct gauge.

DOUBLE MOSS STITCH

Rnds 1 and 2: *K2, P2, rep from * around.
Rnds 3 and 4: *P2, K2, rep from * around.
Rep rnds 1–4.

BODY

THIS PULLOVER is knit in the round. With color A, CO 144 (152, 156, 168) sts. Purl 1 round, knit 1 round. Beg double moss st patt and cont until garment measures 8 (8½, 9, 9½)". Divide sts for front and back. Place back 72 (76, 78, 84) sts on st holder. Work in patt on front 72 (76, 78, 84) sts until front measures 10 (11, 11½, 12)". Beg front neck and shoulder shaping.

FRONT NECK AND SHOULDER SHAPING

CONT IN patt across 23 (24, 25, 26) sts. Place ctr 26 (28, 28, 32) sts on st holder. Join second ball of yarn and work rem 23 (24, 25, 26) sts. Work both shoulders, dec 1 st at neck edge every row 5 times. When front measures 12 (13, 14, 15)", BO 18 (19, 20, 21) sts for each shoulder or place on st holder for 3-needle BO.

BACK

PU BACK sts from st holder. Work back as for front, omitting front neck shaping. When back measures 12 (13, 14, 15)", place ctr 36 (38, 38, 42) sts on st holder. BO 18 (19, 20, 21) sts for each shoulder or place on st holder for 3-needle BO. Join front and back shoulders.

SLEEVES

Make 2.
Sleeves are knit from the top down. They are not knit in the round, but we recommend using a circular needle. With RS facing and color A, PU 44 (50, 56, 62) sts evenly around opening. Work in double moss st patt until sleeve measures 9 (10, 11, 13)". On next row, dec 10 (11, 12, 14) sts evenly across row. Work 6 rows of St st for cuff. BO loosely, letting cuff roll back.

NECK EDGING

WITH RS facing, beg at a shoulder seam and PU 80 (84, 88, 92) sts around neck opening (including sts on st holders). Place marker to designate beg of rnd, and join ends. Knit 4 rnds. BO loosely, letting neck edge roll over.

FINISHING

Sew sleeve seams together. Lightly block pullover. Embroider stems and sew red buttons on front, left sleeve, and back right shoulder. (See "Buttons" on page 22 and "Embroidery" on page 22.)

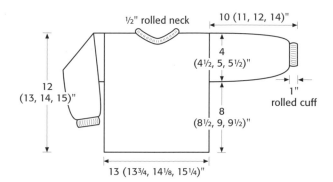

MATERIALS

- Tahki Cotton Classic II, 50-gram skeins (74 yds), 100% cotton

  Color A: 2997 Red   3 skeins
  Color B: 2764 Green   a small amount

- Size 10 circular needle (24")
- Medium-sized crochet hook
- Tapestry needle
- 2 red buttons, ¾" diameter (backpack buttons shown are by LaMode)

GAUGE

12 STITCHES and 20 rows = 4" in pattern stitch.

DIRECTIONS

WITH 2 strands of color A, CO 40 sts. Work double moss st patt (see page 55) until bag measures 18". BO sts.

FINISHING

Fold bag in half. Sew side seams together. Turn bag right side out. With a single strand of color A, single crochet around top edge of bag. To create handles, crochet 2 chains approx 16" long with a single strand of color A. Sew each end to top and bottom of side seams. To create drawstring, crochet 1 chain approx 30" long with a single strand of color B. Weave drawstring through top of backpack 1" from edge. Create 2 tassels by cutting six 7" strands of color B for each tassel. Fold the strands in half. Using tail of yarn from chain, loop through fold and wrap around several times. Sew buttons on where tassels are attached. Trim tassel ends even.

Backpack

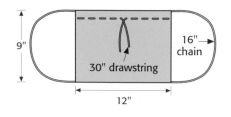

FINISHED MEASUREMENTS

9" x 12" (18" x 12" unfolded)

B' Buzzin' Pullover

$\mathcal{N}$eed we say more? Worked in traditional black and yellow, this pullover will be a conversation piece wherever the lively busy bee who wears it goes. The bottom hemmed channel and drawstring add a touch of style to this easy-fitting pullover.

This pattern is sized 2T (4T, 6, 8).

•

FINISHED MEASUREMENTS

Chest Width: 24 (28, 31, 34)"
Length: 13 (14½, 16, 17½)"
Sleeve Length: 10 (12, 13, 14)"

MATERIALS

- Skacels Polo, 50-gram skeins (153 yds) 60% cotton, 40% acrylic

  Color A: 09 Black   2 (3, 3, 4) skeins
  Color B: 46 Yellow   2 (2, 3, 3) skeins
- Size 6 circular needle (24")
- Size 5 circular needle (24") or dpn for I-cord drawstring
- Stitch holders
- 2 ball-shaped buttons, ⅜" diameter
- Yarn needle

GAUGE

20 STITCHES and 32 rows = 4" in pattern stitch on size 6 needle. To save time, always check your gauge. If necessary, change needle size to obtain correct gauge.

HEM

THE HEM of this pullover forms a channel for the I-cord drawstring. For a nicer finish, this part of the pullover is knit in the round. With size 6 needle and color A, CO 122 (140, 158, 176) sts. Place marker to designate beg of rnd, and join ends.

Rnds 1–5: Knit.

Rnd 6: Purl (turning ridge).

Rnds 7 and 8: Knit.

Rnd 9: *Create buttonholes for drawstring openings:*
     K26 (30, 35, 39) sts, K3tog, YO 2 times, K3 (4, 3, 4) sts, YO 2 times, K3tog, K26 (30, 35, 39) sts. Cont on 61 (70, 79, 88) sts around to marker.

Rnds 10 and 11: Knit.

BOTTOM BORDER DESIGN

AT THE completion of rnd 11, discontinue knitting in the round. At marker indicating the end of rnd 11, beg working back and forth on needle in the traditional manner on bottom border design.

Row 1 (RS): Color A, knit across row, dec 2 sts in row for each size—120 (138, 156, 174) sts.

Row 2 (WS): Color B, purl.

Row 3: Color A, knit.

Row 4: Color A, purl.

Rows 5–7: Work border patt in St st in colors as indicated on graph 1 (see page 60).

Row 8: Color A, purl.

Row 9: Color A, knit across row, inc 2 sts in row for each size—122 (140, 158, 176) sts.

Row 10: Color A, purl.

FRONT

DIVIDE STS for front and back. With RS facing, keep 61 (70, 79, 88) sts on the working needle and place the back 61 (70, 79, 88) sts on st holder. The body of this garment is worked in a 9 st by 12 row patt, alternating color B and color A at 12 row intervals (see graph 2 on page 60). When front measures 11½ (13, 14½, 15½)" from hem turning ridge, ending on WS row, beg front neck and shoulder shaping.

FRONT NECK AND SHOULDER SHAPING

Work in patt across 19 (21, 24, 27) sts. Place ctr 23 (28, 31, 34) sts on st holder. Join second ball of yarn and work rem 19 (21, 24, 27) sts. Work both shoulders, dec on WS rows 1 st at neck edge EOR 3 times. When front measures 13 (14½, 16, 17½)" from hem turning ridge, BO 16 (18, 21, 24) sts for each shoulder or place on st holder for 3-needle BO.

BACK

PU sts from st holder and work in same 9 st by 12 row patt as for front until back measures 12½ (14, 15½, 17)" from hem turning ridge. Work in patt across 17 (19, 22, 25) sts. Place ctr 27 (32, 35, 38) sts on st holder. Work in patt across rem 17 (19, 22, 25) sts. Work both shoulders, dec 1 st at neck edge one time until each shoulder matches front shoulder. BO 16 (18, 21, 24) sts for each shoulder or place on st holder for 3-needle BO. Join front and back shoulders.

SLEEVES

Make 2.

Sleeves are worked from the top down. They are not knit in the round, but we recommend using a circular needle. Place markers 4 (4½, 5, 5)" from shoulder seam on front and back. With RS facing and color B, PU 43 (52, 61, 61) sts evenly between markers. Next row, purl. Switch to color A, beg graph 2 patt (see page 60). Next 12 rows, work 4 rows in color B, 4 rows in color A, and 4 rows in color B. Alternate 12-row black stripe and 12-row black and yellow stripe until sleeve measures 9 (11, 12, 13)", ending on RS row. Next row, purl, dec 5 (7, 9, 9) sts evenly across row. With contrasting color for cuff, work 8 rows in St st on rem 38 (45, 52, 52) sts. BO loosely. Let cuff roll to right side of sleeve.

NECK EDGING

With RS facing, beg at a shoulder seam, PU and purl 74 (82, 90, 98) sts around neck opening including those on st holders. Work in St st for 10 rnds. BO loosely.

I-CORD DRAWSTRING

WITH SIZE 5 circular needle or dpn and color B, CO 2 sts. Knit these 2 sts. Do not turn work. Keeping yarn in back of needle, slide sts to other end of needle and knit. Do not turn work. Again with yarn in back, slide sts to other end of needle. (It helps to pull drawstring downward as you work to even out the sts.) Rep these steps until drawstring measures 38 (42, 48, 54)". BO sts.

B' Buzzin', Graph 1

Work 6 st x 3 row design in St st.

B' Buzzin', Graph 2

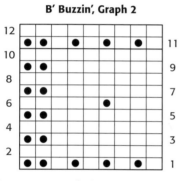

Work 9 st x 12 row design as follows:

☐ St st (Knit on RS rows, purl on WS rows.)

⊡ Purl on RS rows. Row 6 only, ⊡ is a knit st.

Front and back: Work first in color B and next repeat in color A. Work repeats of color B and color A until required measurement.

Sleeves: Work first repeat in color A. For next 12 rows, work 4 rows in color B, 4 in color A, and 4 in color B. Alternate 12-row black stripe and 12-row black and yellow stripe until required measurement.

FINISHING

SEW NECK edging seam together. Sew side seams and sleeve seams together, taking care to match stripes. Fold first 5 rows to WS at hem turning ridge to form bottom hem and create a channel for the drawstring. Insert ends of drawstring through the front openings from the WS. On the WS, sew down the turned-under hem loosely with a yarn needle. At the same time, lay the I-cord drawstring into the channel as you sew.

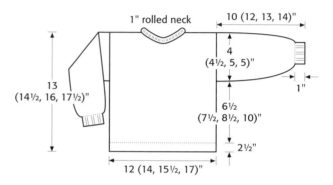

Tickle Me Pink Pullover

𝓘t's cuddles and kisses for the cutie who receives this pullover, which has lots of textured stitches for variety and is knitted in heavy-weight cotton for a quick project. It has the ultimate cozy-cotton feel for a princess all dressed in pink!

This pattern is sized 2T (4T, 6, 8).

•

FINISHED MEASUREMENTS

Chest: 26 (28, 30, 32)"
Length: 13 (14, 15, 16)"
Drop Sleeve: 10 (12, 14, 15)"

MATERIALS

- 6 (7, 8, 9) skeins Tahki Cotton Classic II, 50-gram skeins (74 yds), 100% cotton; color 2446 Pink
- Size 8 circular needle (24")
- Stitch holders
- Medium-sized crochet hook
- Tapestry needle
- 1 small pink button, ½" diameter

GAUGE

18 STITCHES and 24 rows = 4" in pattern stitch. To save time, always check your gauge. If necessary, change needle size to obtain correct gauge.

STITCH PATTERNS

Double Moss Stitch

Rnds 1 and 2: *K2, P2, rep from * around.
Rnds 3 and 4: *P2, K2, rep from * around.
Rep rnds 1–4.

Baby Cable Ribbing

Rows 1 and 3 (WS): K2, *P2, K2, rep from * across.
Row 2: P2, *K2, P2, rep from * across.
Row 4: P2, *K2tog, but leave on needle, then insert right needle between 2 sts just knit tog and knit the first st again; then sl both sts from needle tog, P2, rep from * across.
Rep rows 1–4.

BODY

THIS PULLOVER is knit in the round. In color A, CO 120 (128, 136, 144) sts. Knit first 3 rounds. Work 4 rnds in a K2, P2 rib. Work in double moss st patt until sweater measures 7½ (7½, 8, 8½)". Knit 1 rnd, purl next 2 rnds. Beg knit-purl diamond design (see graph 1 on page 63). After diamonds are completed, purl 2 rnds, and then knit 1 rnd. Divide sts for front and back. Place back 60 (64, 68, 72) sts on st holder. On front 60 (64, 68, 72) sts, work first and last 16 (16, 18, 20) sts in baby cable ribbing patt. Work ctr 28 (32, 32, 32) sts as follows: Work 7 (9, 9, 9) sts in St st, work knit-purl diamond design (see graph 2 on page 63), work 7 (9, 9, 9) sts in St st. When front measures 11 (11½, 12½, 13)", beg neck and shoulder shaping.

FRONT NECK AND SHOULDER SHAPING

CONT IN patt across 19 (20, 21, 22) sts. Place ctr 22 (24, 26, 28) sts on st holder. Join second ball of yarn and work rem 19 (20, 21, 22) sts. Work both shoulders in patt, dec 1 st at neck edge every row 4 times. When front measures 13 (14, 15, 16)", BO 15 (16, 17, 18) sts for each shoulder or place on st holder for 3-needle BO.

BACK

PU STS from st holder, work in baby cable ribbing patt as for front, omitting St st and diamond design on ctr sts, and neck shaping, until back measures 13 (14, 15, 16)". BO 15 (16, 17, 18) sts for each shoulder or place on st holder for 3-needle BO, and place ctr 30 (32, 34, 36) sts on st holder. Join front and back shoulders.

SLEEVES

Make 2.
Sleeves are knit from the top down. They are not knit in the round, but we recommend using a circular needle. With RS facing and color A, PU 40 (50, 56, 60) sts evenly around opening. Work sleeve in St st except for ctr 6 sts, which are worked in baby cable ribbing as for front (on RS row, P2, K2, P2). Cont in patt until sleeve measures 9 (11, 13, 14)". Next row, dec 10 (12, 14, 14) sts evenly across row. Work 6 rows of K2, P2 rib for cuff. BO cuff in K2, P2.

TURTLENECK

WITH RS facing and color A, beg at a shoulder seam and PU 70 (78, 82, 90) sts around neck opening, including sts on st holders. Place marker to designate beg of rnd, and join ends. Work in the rnd in K2, P2, rib for 3" to 4". BO in K2, P2. Fold neck over.

FINISHING

SEW SLEEVE seams together. Single crochet around hem of pullover and turtleneck edge. Make French knots in the ctr of each small diamond. In the ctr of large diamond, slide a small button through the needle first before making your French knot.

Tickle Me Pink, Graph 1

Work 8 st x 7 row design as follows:
- ⊙ Reverse St st (Purl on RS, knit on WS.)
- ☐ St st (Knit on RS, purl on WS.)

Tickle Me Pink, Graph 2

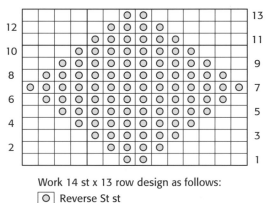

Work 14 st x 13 row design as follows:
- ⊙ Reverse St st
- ☐ St st

Work 7 (9, 9, 9) sts each side of graph.

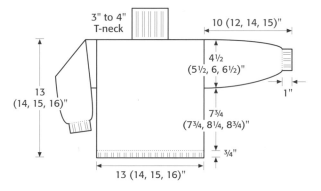

3" to 4" T-neck

10 (12, 14, 15)"

4½ (5½, 6, 6½)"

13 (14, 15, 16)"

7¾ (7¾, 8¼, 8¾)"

1"

¾"

13 (14, 15, 16)"

Flower Power Pullover

$\mathcal{T}$he retro 70s look is everywhere, and this easy pullover shows it off well with little effort.
Flower button embellishments really jazz it up. What child won't love modeling this work of art?

GAUGE

22 STITCHES and 28 rows = 4" in pattern stitch. To save time, always check your gauge. If necessary, change needle size to obtain correct gauge.

DOUBLE MOSS STITCH

Rnds 1 and 2: *K2, P2, rep from * around.
Rnds 3 and 4: *P2, K2, rep from * around.
Rep rnds 1–4.

BODY

THIS SWEATER is knit in the round. With color A, CO 144 (152, 156, 168) sts. Rnd 1: Purl. Rnd 2: Knit. Beg double moss st patt and work until garment measures 8 (8½, 9, 9½)". Divide sts for front and back. Place back 72 (76, 78, 84) sts on st holder. Work front 72 (76, 78, 84) sts in patt until front measures 10 (11, 11½, 12)". Beg front neck and shoulder shaping.

This pattern is sized 2T (3T, 4T, 6).

●

FINISHED MEASUREMENTS

Chest: 26 (27½, 28¼, 30½)"
Length: 12 (13, 14, 15)"
Drop Sleeve: 10 (11, 12, 14)"

FRONT NECK AND SHOULDER SHAPING

WORK IN patt across 23 (24, 25, 26) sts, and place ctr 26 (28, 28, 32) sts on st holder. Join yarn and work in patt across rem 23 (24, 25, 26) sts. Work both shoulders in patt, dec 1 st at neck edge every row 5 times. When front measures 12 (13, 14, 15)", BO 18 (19, 20, 21) sts for each shoulder or place on st holder for 3-needle BO.

MATERIALS

- 4 (5, 6, 7) skeins Tahki Cotton Classic, 50-gram skeins (108 yds), 100% cotton, #3001 White
- Size 6 circular needle (24")
- Stitch holders
- Tapestry needle
- 2 packages flower buttons, ⅝" diameter (garment buttons shown are by Dress It Up)
- 2 bumblebee buttons, ¾" diameter (garment buttons shown are by JHB)

BACK

PU BACK sts from st holder. Work back same as front, omitting front neck shaping. When back measures 12 (13, 14, 15)", BO 18 (19, 20, 21) sts for each shoulder or place on st holder for 3-needle BO, and place ctr 36 (38, 38, 42) sts on st holder. Join front and back shoulders.

SLEEVES

Make 2.

Sleeves are knit from the top down. They are not knit in the round, but we recommend using a circular needle. With RS facing and color A, PU 44 (50, 56, 62) sts evenly around opening. Work sleeve in double moss st patt as for front until sleeve measures 9 (10, 11, 13)". On next row, dec 10 (11, 12, 14) sts evenly across row. Work 6 rows of St st for cuff. BO.

NECK EDGING

With RS facing and color A, beg at a shoulder seam and PU 80 (84, 88, 92) sts around neck opening, including those sts on st holders. Place marker to designate beg of rnd, and join ends. Knit 4 rnds. BO loosely, letting neck roll over.

FINISHING

Sew sleeve seams together. Lightly block pullover. Sew flower buttons all over pullover front, back, and sleeves any way you wish. Be creative! Have fun!

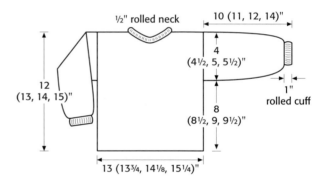

Moo Moo Pullover

𝒯his pullover is a real barnyard bonanza! It's a great zippered, superwash wool pullover for a young milk drinker you know. A decorative cow zipper pull inspired the name for the project. The pullover was designed to coordinate with both "Choo Choo Pullover with Hat" (page 70) and "Rush Hour Cardigan" (page 80) so that the whole family can look fabulous.

This pattern is sized 2T (4T, 6, 8).

•

FINISHED MEASUREMENTS

Chest: 26 (28½, 30, 32½)"
Length: 13 (14¼, 15, 16)"
Drop Sleeve: 10 (12, 14, 15)"

MATERIALS

- Filatura Di Crosa Primo, 50-gram skeins
  (76½ yds), 100% superwash wool

  Color A: Pink   4 (5, 6, 7) skeins
  Color B: Black   1 (1, 1, 1) skein
  Color C: White   1 (1, 1, 1) skein

- Size 9 circular needle (24")
- Stitch holders
- Medium-sized crochet hook
- 7" jumbo zipper in black
- Decorative zipper pull (zipper pull shown is
  from Trendsetter)
- Sewing needle and black thread
- Yarn needle

GAUGE

16 STITCHES and 20 rows = 4" in pattern stitch. To save time, always check your gauge. If necessary, change needle size to obtain correct gauge.

BODY

THIS PULLOVER is knit in the round. With color B, CO 104 (114, 120, 130) sts. Place marker to designate beg of rnd, and join ends.

Rnd 1: Purl.
Rnd 2: Knit
Rnd 3: Purl.
Beg checkerboard patt.
Rnds 4 and 5: *K2 in color B, K2 in color C, rep from * around.
Rnds 6 and 7: *K2 in color C, K2 in color B, rep from * around.
Rnds 8 and 9: Rep rnds 4 and 5.
Rnd 10: Color B, knit.
Rnd 11: Color B, purl.

With color A, knit rnds until pullover measures 3 (3H, 4, 5)". On next rnd, beg graph design (see page 69) on 14 sts of ctr front. At appropriate point in graph, divide sts for back and 2 front sections. Place back 52 (58, 60, 66) sts on st holder. Join second ball of yarn and work each set of 26 (28, 30, 32) sts in patt until front measures 11 (11H, 12, 13)". Beg front neck and shoulder shaping.

FRONT NECK AND SHOULDER SHAPING

BO 6 (7, 8, 8) sts at neck edge. Cont in patt, dec 1 st at neck edge every row 3 times. When front measures 13 (14¼, 15, 16)", BO 17 (18, 19, 21) sts for each shoulder or place on st holder for 3-needle BO.

BACK

PU sts from st holder and work in St st in color A as for front, omitting the zipper, checkerboard, and neck shaping, until back measures 13 (14¼, 15, 16)". BO 17 (18, 19, 21) sts for each shoulder or place on st holder for 3-needle BO, and place ctr 18 (22, 22, 24) sts on st holder. Join front and back shoulders.

SLEEVES

Make 2.

SLEEVES ARE knit from the top down. They are not knit in the round, but we recommend using a circular needle. Place marker 4 (4½, 5, 5½)" from shoulder seam on front and back. With RS facing and color A, PU 40 (44, 50, 54) sts evenly between markers. Work in St st until sleeve measures 8 (10,

12, 13)". Next (RS) row: With color B, knit across, dec 10 (12, 12, 14) sts evenly across row. Next row: Purl. At this point, rep checkerboard design as for body. Purl final row in color B. BO sts.

COLLAR

WITH WS facing and color A, beg at the left edge of placket and PU 54 (60, 62, 66) sts around neck opening, including sts on st holder. Work back and forth on needle in K1, P1 ribbing for 2" to 2½". BO sts in patt.

FINISHING

SEW SLEEVE seams together. Lightly block pullover. With RS facing, place zipper so that the teeth show in front opening. Pin zipper securely. Turn garment to wrong side and hand sew zipper with regular cotton thread. At collar edge, tuck and secure zipper tabs under, toward the wrong side of the garment. In color C, single crochet around hem of pullover. In color B, single crochet around collar. Attach decorative zipper pull.

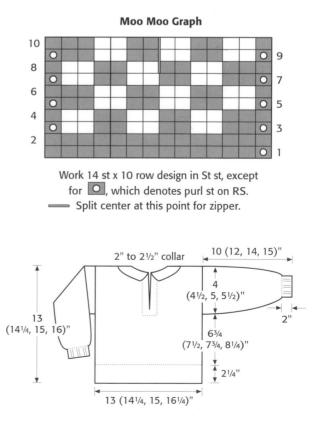

Moo Moo Graph

Work 14 st x 10 row design in St st, except for ▢, which denotes purl st on RS.
⎯ Split center at this point for zipper.

Choo Choo Pullover
with Hat

*T*rains are popular among little kids, and they'll love the train button on the front of this cheerful pullover. Dressed in this superwash wool V-neck with matching hat, budding engineers can climb aboard their own imaginary train!

Pullover

This pattern is sized 2T (4T, 6, 8).

●

FINISHED MEASUREMENTS

Chest: 26 (28½, 30, 32½)"
Length: 13 (14, 15, 16)"
Drop Sleeve: 10 (12, 14, 15)"

MATERIALS

- Filatura Di Crosa Primo, 50-gram skeins (76½ yds.), 100% superwash wool

  Color A: Blue   4 (5, 6, 7) skeins
  Color B: Green   1 (1, 1, 1) skein

- Size 9 circular needle (24")
- Stitch holders
- Medium-sized crochet hook
- 1 decorative button, 1¼" diameter (garment button shown is by LaMode)
- Yarn needle

GAUGE

16 STITCHES and 20 rows = 4" in pattern stitch. To save time, always check your gauge. If necessary, change needle size to obtain correct gauge.

BODY

THIS PULLOVER is knit in the round. With color A, CO 105 (115, 120, 130) sts. Place marker to designate beg of rnd, and join ends. Work first 3 rounds in seed st (see page 20). Beg wide rib patt.
Rnd 1: Knit.
Rnd 2: *K4, P1, rep from * around.
Rep these 2 rnds until pullover measures 5H (6, 6H, 7)". Cont in patt, beg stripes: Work 2 rows in color B, 8 rows in color A, 4 rows in color B, 1 row in color A. To mark ctr front for V neck, count sts and mark halfway point; then on one section, count sts and mark halfway point again, and place marker.

V NECK

WORKING BACK and forth on the needle, cont in wide rib patt, working K2tog on each edge of marker EOR, until garment measures 8½ (9, 9½, 10)". Divide sts for back and 2 fronts. Place back 53 (57, 60, 66) sts on st holder. Join second ball of yarn and work both front sections, dec 1 st at neck edge EOR 6 times. With color A, work in patt, dec 1 st at neck edge every row until there are 9 (10, 11, 12) sts rem for each shoulder. When front measures 13 (14, 15, 16)", BO sts for each shoulder or place on st holder for 3-needle BO.

BACK

PU STS from st holder and work in wide rib and stripe patt as for front, omitting neck shaping until back measures 13 (14, 15, 16)". BO 9 (10, 11, 12) sts for each shoulder or place on st holder for 3-needle BO, and place ctr 35 (37, 38, 42) sts on st holder. Join front and back shoulders.

SLEEVES

Make 2.

Sleeves are knit from the top down. They are not knit in the round, but we recommend using a circular needle. With RS facing and color A, PU 40 (45, 45, 50) sts evenly around opening. Work in wide rib until sleeve measures 6 (8, 10, 11)". Work 4 rows in color B. Cont in patt in color A until sleeve measures 9 (11, 13, 14)". Dec 10 (11, 11, 14) sts evenly across next row. Work 5 rows of seed st for cuff. BO cuff.

NECK EDGING

WITH RS facing and color B, beg at the point of the V, and PU 112 (114, 116, 120) sts around neck opening, including sts on st holder. Work back and forth on the needle in seed st for 2½" to 3". BO sts in patt.

FINISHING

SEW SLEEVE seams together. With RS facing, lay left side of neck ribbing over right and tack down with a decorative button; refer to photo on page 71. With color B, single crochet around hem of pullover and sleeve cuffs. Block pullover carefully.

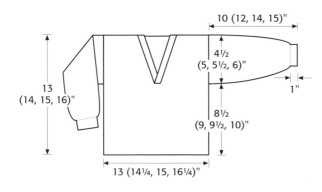

Hat

This pattern is sized Small (Medium, Large).

●

FINISHED MEASUREMENTS

Circumference: 15¾ (19¼, 21)"

MATERIALS

- Filatura Di Crosa Primo, 50-gram skeins (76½ yds) 100% superwash wool

  Color A: Blue   1 (1, 1) skein
  Color B: Green   1 (1, 1) skein
  Color C: Yellow   1 (1, 1) skein

- Size 9 circular needle (16")
- Yarn needle

GAUGE

16 STITCHES and 20 rows = 4" in pattern stitch.

DIRECTIONS

THE HAT is knit in the round.

With color A, CO 63 (77, 84) sts. Work 8 rounds in K1, P1 rib. Work in patt and color sequence as follows:

Color B: 3 (4, 5) rnds.

Color C: 1 rnd.

Next rnd: *K1 in color A, K6 in color C, rep from * around.

Next rnd: K2 in color A, K4 in color C, *K3 in color A, K4 in color C, rep from * around to last st, end K1 in color A.

Next rnd: K3 in color A, K2 in color C, *K5 in color A, K2 in color C, rep from * around to last 2 sts, end K2 in color A.

Color A: 5 rnds, dec 1 (3, 2) sts on one of these rnds.

Next rnd: *K1 in color B, sl 1, rep from * around.

Color B: 3 (4, 5) rnds.

Next rnd: *K1 in color C, sl 1, rep from * around.

Color C: 2 rnds

Next rnd: *K1 in color A, sl 1, rep from * around.

Color C: 8 (9, 10) rnds.

Next rnd: *K1 in color A, sl 1, rep from * around.

Color A: 3 rnds.

Color A: K2tog around.

Color A: Rep last rnd 2 times.

BO rem sts and tie together tightly.

POM-POM

To CREATE pom-pom, wind strands of colors A, B, and C around a piece of 4"-wide cardboard until your pom-pom is firm and thick. Slip off cardboard and tie tightly in the middle with separate strand of yarn, leaving long tails. Trim ends even. Fluff pom-pom. Secure to top of hat with tails.

15¾ (19¼, 21)"

Picket Fence Tunic

Grandma's little garden helper will look great in this fancy tunic with embroidered flower embellishments climbing a cleverly knit, white picket fence. A lightweight cotton yarn is perfect for warm summer afternoons.

GAUGE

22 STITCHES and 28 rows = 4" in pattern stitch. To save time, always check your gauge. If necessary, change needle size to obtain correct gauge.

BODY

THIS TUNIC is knit in the round to the armholes. In color A, CO 180 sts (all sizes). Place marker to designate beg of rnd, and join ends.

Rnds 1–3: Work in seed st (page 20).

Rnds 4–9: Knit.

Rnd 10: *Color C, K1, P1, rep from * around.

Rnd 11: *K1 in color C, (the knit sts), K1 in color A, (the purl sts), rep from * around.

Rnd 12: *K1 in color B, P1 in color C, K1 in color B, P1 in color C, K1 in color A, P1 in color C, K1 in color A, P1 in color C, rep from * around.

Rnd 13: *K3 in color B, K1 in color C, K1 in color A, K1 in color C, K1 in color A, K1 in color C, rep from * around.

Rnd 14: Rep rnd 13.

Rnds 15 and 16: Color B, knit.

Rnds 17–19: *K3 in color B, K5 in color A, rep from * around.

Rnds 20 and 21: Color B, knit.

Rnd 22: *K3 in color B, K5 in color A, rep from * around.

Rnd 23: *K1 in color B, K7 in color A, rep from * around.

In color A, knit rnds until garment measures 8 (10, 11)". On next rnd, K2tog every 5 (9, 9) sts. Divide sts for front and back. Place back 72 (80, 80) sts on st holder. Working on front 72 (80, 80) sts, beg seed st. As you work across first row, only on size 3T, K2tog at each end, leaving 72 (78, 80) sts on needle. Cont in seed st until front measures 10 (12, 13)". Beg V-neck shaping.

This pattern is sized 2T (3T, 4T).

•

FINISHED MEASUREMENTS

Chest: 26 (28, 29)"
Length: 13 (15, 17)"
Sleeve: 2 (2½, 3)"

MATERIALS

- Tahki Cotton Classic, 50-gram skeins (108 yds), 100% cotton

Color A: 3839 Blue	6 (7, 8) skeins
Color B: 3001 White	1 (1, 1) skein
Color C: 3764 Green	1 (1, 1) skein
Color D: 3533 Yellow	a small amount
Color E: 3459 Pink	a small amount
Color F: 3402 Orange	a small amount

- Size 6 circular needle (24")
- Stitch holders
- Tapestry needle
- Medium-sized crochet hook

V-NECK SHAPING

CONT IN patt across 36 (39, 40) sts. Join yarn and work in patt across 36 (39, 40) sts. Work both shoulders in patt, dec 1 st at neck edge every row until 18 (20, 20) sts rem on needle for each shoulder. BO sts for each shoulder or place on st holder for 3-needle BO.

BACK

PU BACK sts from st holder. Work across first row in seed st, only for size 3T, K2tog at each end. Work back as for front, omitting front neck shaping. When back measures 13 (15, 17)", BO 18 (19, 20) sts for each shoulder or place on st holder for 3-needle BO, and place ctr 36 (40, 40) sts on st holder. Join front and back shoulders.

SLEEVES

Make 2.
Sleeves are knit from the top down. They are not knit in the round, but we recommend using a circular needle. Place markers 4 (4½, 5)" from shoulder seam on front and back. With RS facing and color A, PU 44 (50, 55) sts evenly between markers. Work in St st until sleeve measures 1¾ (2¼, 2¾)". Next row: Dec 12 (14, 16) sts evenly across row. Work 3 rows of seed st for cuff. BO.

NECK EDGING

WITH COLOR B, CO 55 sts; then with RS facing, beg at ctr of V-neck opening and PU 90 (94, 104) sts around neck opening, including sts on st holders. Then CO another 55 sts. Work 5 rows of seed st. BO.

FINISHING

SEW SLEEVE seams and small side-seam opening together. Lightly block sweater. With color C, single crochet around bottom hem and sleeve cuffs. Refer to "Embroidery" on page 22. Embroider flowers in lazy daisy st. Make French knot ctrs. Embroider stems and leaves as shown.

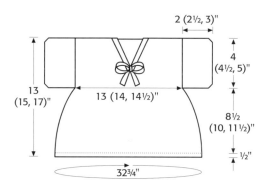

Patchwork Pansies Cardigan

$\mathcal{D}$esigned to coordinate with "Picket Fence Tunic," this lightweight cotton cardigan is a perfect complement to any girl's spring and summer wardrobe. We embroidered the pansies to add creative flair and a bit of fun. A single button closure keeps the cardigan design simple.

This pattern is sized 2T (4T, 6).

●

FINISHED MEASUREMENTS

Chest: 26 (28, 30)"
Length: 13 (15, 16)"
Drop Sleeve: 10 (12, 14)"

MATERIALS

- Tahki Cotton Classic, 50-gram skeins
  (108 yds), 100% cotton

Color A: 3533 Yellow	4 (6, 7) skeins
Color B: 3459 Pink	a small amount
Color C: 3764 Green	a small amount
Color D: 3402 Orange	a small amount
Color E: 3726 Lime	a small amount
Color F: 3808 Blue	a small amount
Color G: 3947 Purple	a small amount

- Size 6 circular needle (24")
- Stitch holders
- 1 bee button, ¾" diameter (garment button
  shown is by JHB)
- Tapestry needle

GAUGE

22 STITCHES and 28 rows = 4" in pattern stitch. To save time, always check your gauge. If necessary, change needle size to obtain correct gauge.

BODY

THIS CARDIGAN is not knit in the round, but we recommend using a circular needle and working the garment in one piece to the armholes. With color A, CO 128 (136, 144) sts. Work rows 1–5 (1–11, 1–16) in seed st (see page 20). Next row (RS): Beg patchwork blocks. (Note: For all sizes, each block is 12 sts by 16 rows with 6 sts between blocks, all in St st.) Work 4 (8, 12) sts in seed st in color A, K12 in color B (first block), K6 in color A, K12 in color E, K6 in color A, K12 in color F, K6 in color A, K12 in color B, K6 in color A, K12 in color C, K6 in color A, K12 in color D, K6 in color A, K12 in color G, work last 4 (8, 12) sts in seed st in color A. Cont in patt until 16 rows of block patt are complete. Next row: With color A, beg cardigan body patt.

Rows 1, 3, and 5 (RS): Work 4 (8, 12) sts in seed st, knit across, end last 4 (8, 12) sts in seed st.

Rows 2, 4, and 6 (WS): Work 4 (8, 12) sts in seed st, *K12, P6, rep from * across, end last 4 (8, 12) sts in seed st.

Rows 7, 9, and 11 (RS): Work 4 (8, 12) sts in seed st, knit across, end last 4 (8, 12) sts in seed st.

Rows 8 and 10: Work 4 (8, 12) in seed st, K3, *P6, K12, rep from * across, end K3, 4 (8, 12) sts in seed st.

Row 12: Rep row 8.

Rep these 12 rows to create this woven patt.

Cont in patt until garment measures 9 (10, 10½)". Divide sts for back and fronts. Place back 64 (68, 72) sts on st holder. Join yarn and work 32 (34, 36) sts for each front at same time in patt until front measures 11 (13, 13½)". Beg front neck and shoulder shaping.

FRONT NECK AND SHOULDER SHAPING

WORKING BOTH fronts, BO 6 (7, 8) sts at neck edge, cont in patt across rem 26 (27, 28) sts. Work both shoulders in patt, dec 1 st at neck edge every row 6 times. When front measures 13 (15, 16)", BO 20 (21, 22) sts for each shoulder or place on st holder for 3-needle BO.

BACK

PU BACK sts from st holder. Work back as for front, omitting front neck shaping, until back measures 13 (15, 16)". BO 20 (21, 22) sts for each shoulder or place sts on st holder for 3-needle BO, and place ctr 24 (26, 28) sts on st holder. Join front and back shoulders.

SLEEVES

Make 2.
Sleeves are knit from the top down. They are not knit in the round, but we recommend using a circular needle. With RS facing and color A, PU 46 (56, 62) sts evenly around opening. Work in garter st until sleeve measures 9 (11, 13)". Next row, dec 10 (12, 14) sts evenly across row. Work 2" of seed st for cuff. BO loosely. Fold cuff over.

RUFFLED COLLAR

WITH RS facing, beg at edge of right placket and PU 60 (62, 72) sts around neck opening, including those sts on st holder. Work 8 rows of St st. Create ruffle by inc 2 sts in each st on next row. Work next 4 rows in K4, P4 ribbing. BO in K4, P4.

FINISHING

SEW SLEEVE seams together. Lightly block cardigan. Crochet a chain about 2" long for the buttonhole. Secure to right placket about 2" from neck edge. Sew on bee button to left placket. Tack down collar in front if needed. Use the lazy daisy st to embroider 1 flower in each block and on the back, just below the neck and between the shoulders. With a contrasting color, make a French knot in the ctr of each flower. See "Embroidery" on page 22.

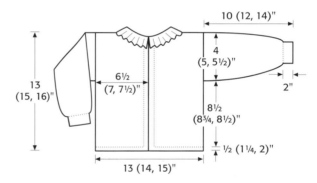

Rush Hour Cardigan

$\mathcal{H}$onk, honk! Beep, beep! It's time to go cruising around town sporting a dynamic zippered cardigan. Here's another terrific unisex sweater to coordinate with both "Moo Moo Pullover" (page 67) and "Choo Choo Pullover with Hat" (page 70).

This pattern is sized 4T (6, 8).

●

FINISHED MEASUREMENTS

Chest: 30 (32 ½, 35)"
Length: 15 (16, 17)"
Drop Sleeve: 12 (14, 15)"

MATERIALS

- Filatura Di Crosa Primo, 50-gram skeins
  (76½ yds), 100% superwash wool

Color A: Blue	1 (1, 2) skeins
Color B: Pink	4 (4, 5) skeins
Color C: Green	1 (1, 2) skeins
Color D: Yellow	2 (3, 4) skeins
Color E: Black	1 (1, 1) skein

- Size 9 circular needle (24")
- Stitch holders
- Medium-sized crochet hook
- 12 (12, 14)" jumbo-sized zipper (zipper for
  model garment is pink)
- Yarn needle
- Sewing needle and black thread

GAUGE

16 STITCHES and 20 rows = 4" in pattern stitch. To save time, always check your gauge. If necessary, change needle size to obtain correct gauge.

BODY

THIS CARDIGAN is not knit in the round, but we recommend using a circular needle and working the garment in one piece to armholes. With color E, CO 120 (130, 140) sts.

Rows 1–9: K1, P1, rib across.
Row 10: Color C, purl.
Row 11: Color B, *K1, sl 1 wyif, rep from * across.
Row 12: Color B, purl.
Row 13: Color B, knit.
Row 14: Color A, *P1, sl 1 wyif, rep from * across.
Row 15: Color B, knit.
Row 16: Color B, purl.
Row 17: Color A, *K1, sl 1 wyib, rep from * across.
Rows 18–21: Color A, work in St st.
Row 22: Color D, purl.
Beg triangle patt.
Row 23: *K1 in color C, K9 in color D, rep from * across.
Row 24: P2 in color C, *P7 in color D, P3 in color C, rep from * across, end P7 in color D, P1 in color C.
Row 25: K3 in color C, *K5 in color D, K5 in color C, rep from * across, end K5 in color D, K2 in color C.
Row 26: P4 in color C, *P3 in color D, P7 in color C, rep from * across, end P3 in color D, P3 in color C.
Row 27: K5 in color C, *K1 in color D, K9 in color C, rep from * across, end K1 in color D, K4 in color C.
Row 28: Color C, purl.
Row 29: Color A, knit.
Row 30: *P1 in color C, sl 1 wyif, rep from * across.
Row 31: Color C, knit.
Row 32: Color B, purl.
Row 33: Color B, knit.

Row 34: *P1 in color D, P1 in color C, rep from * across.

Row 35: Color E, knit.

Row 36: *P1 in color C, sl 1 wyib, rep from * across.

Row 38: Color D, purl.

Row 39: Color A, knit.

Row 40: Color A, purl.

Beg four-color mix patt.

Multiple of 4 sts plus 3

Row 1 (RS): Color B, K1, *sl 1 wyib, K3, rep from *, end sl 1, K1.

Row 2: Color C, P3, *sl 1 wyif, P3, rep from * across.

Row 3: Color D, rep row 1.

Row 4: Color B, rep row 2.

Row 5: Color A, rep row 1.

Row 6: Color D, rep row 2.

Row 7: Color C, rep row 1.

Row 8: Color A, rep row 2.

Rep rows 1–8.

Cont in four-color mix patt until garment measures 10 (11, 12)". Divide for back and fronts. Place back 60 (66, 70) sts on st holder. Join second ball of yarn and work 30 (32, 35) sts for each front. Work St st as follows: 2 rows in color A, 1 row in color D. Work 1 row of K1, P1 rib across in color B. Work in St st until front measures 12 (13, 14)". Beg front neck and shoulder shaping.

FRONT NECK AND SHOULDER SHAPING

FOR EACH front, BO 6 (7, 8) sts at neck edge.

Left shoulder: Cont in B, dec 1 st at neck edge every row 4 times until front measures 15 (16, 17)". BO 20 (21, 23) sts for shoulder or place on st holder for 3-needle BO.

Right shoulder:

Row 1 (WS): Color C, purl.

Row 2: Color C, knit.

Row 3: Color A, *P1, sl 1 wyib, rep from * across.

Row 4: Color A, knit.

Row 5: Color B, purl.

Row 6: Color B, knit.

Row 7: Color D, *P1, sl 1, rep from * across.

Rows 8–10: Color D, work in St st.

Row 11: Color C, *P1, sl 1, rep from * across.

Row 12: Color D, knit.

Cont in color D St st until front measures 15 (16, 17)". BO 20 (21, 23) sts for shoulder or place on st holder for 3-needle BO.

BACK

PU STS from st holder and cont to work in four-color mix patt until back measures 15 (16, 17)". BO 20 (21, 23) sts for each shoulder or place on st holder for 3-needle BO, and place ctr 20 (24, 24) sts on st holder. Join front and back shoulders.

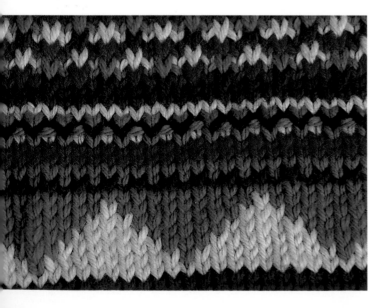

SLEEVES

Make 2.

Sleeves are knit from the top down. They are not knit in the round, but we recommend using a circular needle.

Right sleeve: With RS facing and color B, PU 50 sts (all sizes) evenly around opening. Work in St st until sleeve measures 10½ (12½, 13½)". Next (RS) row, dec 10 sts evenly across row. Change to color E, and work 1½" of K1, P1 rib. BO.

Left sleeve: With color D, work as for right sleeve.

COLLAR

With WS facing and color E, beg at the right edge of right front neck opening and PU 54 (60, 64) sts around neck opening, including sts on st holder. Work back and forth on needle in K1, P1 ribbing for 2". BO sts. Fold collar over in half toward WS and stitch down.

FINISHING

Sew sleeve seams together. With color E, single crochet front edge of placket openings. Lightly block cardigan. With RS facing, place zipper so that the teeth show in front opening. Pin zipper securely. Turn garment to wrong side and hand sew zipper, using regular cotton thread. At collar edge, tuck and secure zipper tabs under, toward the WS of the garment.

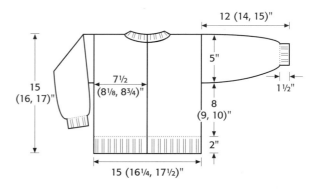

Watermelon Cardigan

*H*ot summer days, picnics at the beach, cool lemonade, and watermelon are all childhood memories of summer. Create some memories for a new generation with this bright and summery cotton cardigan.

DOUBLE MOSS STITCH

Rows 1 and 2: *K2, P2, rep from * across.
Rows 3 and 4: *P2, K2, rep from * across.
Rep rows 1–4.

BODY

THIS CARDIGAN is not knit in the round, but we recommend using a circular needle and working the garment in one piece to armholes. With color A, CO 144 (150, 154, 166) sts. Work the first 6 rows in double moss st. Next RS row, beg stripe patt on right front, work 6 sts in color A in double moss st, work next 66 (68, 70, 76) sts in color B in St st, work rem sts in color A in double moss st. Cont in patt to create 9-row stripes of colors B and C as shown. As you work up right front, place 3 (4, 4, 4) buttonholes, evenly spaced, up right placket every 3 (2⅕, 2¾, 3)", beg 2" from bottom edge and ending 1" from neck edge. Cont until garment measures 8 (8½, 9, 9½)". Divide sts for back and 2 fronts. Place back 72 (74, 78, 82) sts on st holder. Join yarn and work 36 (38, 38, 42) sts for each front in patt until front measures 10 (11, 11½, 12)". Beg front neck and shoulder shaping.

FRONT NECK AND SHOULDER SHAPING

To SHAPE front neckline, BO first 9 (10, 10, 12) sts at each neck edge. Cont in patt across rem 27 (28, 28, 30) sts. Work both shoulders in patt, dec 1 st at neck edge every row 5 (5, 5, 6) times, until front measures 12 (13, 14, 15)". BO 22 (23, 23, 24) sts for each shoulder or place on st holder for 3-needle BO.

This pattern is sized 2T (3T, 4T, 6).

●

FINISHED MEASUREMENTS

Chest: 26 (27, 28, 30)"
Length: 12 (13, 14, 15)"
Drop Sleeve: 10 (11, 12, 14)"

MATERIALS

- Tahki Cotton Classic, 50-gram skeins (108 yds), 100% cotton

Color A: 3001 White	2 (3, 3, 4) skeins
Color B: 3459 Pink	2 (2, 2, 2) skeins
Color C: 3764 Green	2 (2, 2, 2) skeins

- Size 6 circular needle (24")
- Stitch holders
- 3 (4, 4, 4) watermelon buttons, 1" diameter (garment buttons shown are by JHB)
- Yarn needle

GAUGE

22 STITCHES and 28 rows = 4" in pattern stitch. To save time, always check your gauge. If necessary, change needle size to obtain correct gauge.

BACK

PU back sts from st holder. Work back as for front, omitting front neck shaping, until back measures 12 (13, 14, 15)". BO 22 (23, 23, 24) sts for each shoulder or place on st holder for 3-needle BO, and place ctr 28 (28, 32, 34) sts on st holder. Join front and back shoulders.

SLEEVES

Make 2.

Sleeves are knit from the top down. They are not knit in the round, but we recommend using a circular needle.

Right sleeve: With RS facing and color C, PU 44 (50, 56, 62) sts evenly around opening. Work in St st until sleeve measures 9 (10, 11, 13)". Next row, dec 10 (11, 12, 14) sts evenly across row. Work 6 rows of double moss st for cuff. BO.

Left sleeve: With color B, work as for right sleeve.

NECK EDGING

With color A and RS facing, beg at edge of right placket and PU 68 (70, 78, 88) sts around neck opening, including sts on st holder. Work 4 rows of double moss st. BO in patt.

FINISHING

Sew sleeve seams together. Lightly block cardigan. Sew on buttons to left placket.

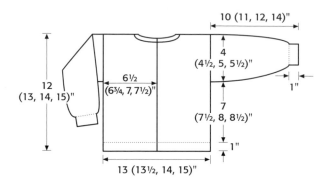

Cat Tales Cardigan

𝓜ice and cats—children find them intriguing. And we think the picot edging, quaint touches of color, and washable wool yarn for this cardigan will intrigue you. Oh, by the way, the mouse gets away!

This pattern is sized 18M (2T, 3T, 4T).

●

FINISHED MEASUREMENTS

Chest: 24 (26, 27, 28)"
Total Length: 12 (13, 14, 15)"
Sleeve Length: 9 (10, 11, 12)"

MATERIALS

- Heirloom Easy Care, 50-gram balls (105 yds), 100% washable wool

Color A: 773 Light Blue	3 (3, 4, 4) skeins
Color B: 777 Dark Blue	1 (1, 2, 2) skeins
Color C: 790 Yellow	1 (1, 1, 1) skeins
Color D: 795 Red	1 (1, 1, 1) skein
Color E: 705 White	1 (1, 1, 1) skein

- Size 6 circular needle (24")
- Stitch holders
- Tapestry needle
- Medium-sized crochet hook
- 5 (5, 6, 6) buttons, ⅝" diameter

GAUGE

24 STITCHES and 30 rows = 4" in stockinette stitch. To save time, always check your gauge. If necessary, change needle size to obtain correct gauge.

BODY

THIS CARDIGAN is not knit in the round, but we recommend using a circular needle and working the garment in one piece to armholes. With color C, CO 148 (156, 164, 172) sts. Beg bottom hem in picot edging.

Row 1 (WS): Purl.
Row 2 (RS): Knit.
Row 3: Purl.
Row 4: (Turning row) K2, *YO, K2tog, rep from * to end.
Row 5: Purl.
Row 6: Knit.
Cont on foll rows for decorative bottom design:
Row 7: Color B, purl.
Row 8: Knit.
Row 9: Color A, K1, P1 across row.
Row 10: Color E, knit.
Row 11: Color A, K1, P1 across row.
Row 12: Knit.

Row 13: Color D, purl.

Row 14: Color C, knit.

Row 15: Color D, purl.

Row 16: Color A, knit.

Row 17: Color C, K1, P1 across row.

Row 18: Color B, knit.

Row 19: Purl.

Beg 6-row checkerboard patt.

Row 20: *K4 in color B, K4 in color E, rep from * to end.

Row 21: *P4 in color B, P4 in color E, rep from * to end.

Row 22: *K4 in color E, K4 in color B, rep from * to end.

Row 23: *P4 in color E, P4 in color B, rep from * to end.

Rows 24 and 25: Rep rows 20 and 21.

Row 26: Color B, knit.

Row 27: Color B, purl.

Row 28: Color C, knit.

Row 29: Color C, purl.

Row 30: Color D, knit.

Row 31: Color A, P1, sl 1, P1, sl 1 to end.

Rows 32–37: Color A, St st for 5 rows. In last row, dec 4 (0, 2, 4) sts evenly in row.

Row 38: Divide sts for back and 2 fronts. Place 36 (39, 40, 42) sts on st holder for right front section. Join second ball of color A and work across back 72 (78, 82, 84) sts. Place rem 36 (39, 40, 42) sts on st holder for left front.

BACK

Cont in color A and St st until back measures 4½ (5, 5½, 6)" from beg. Next RS row, cont in St st across 13 (16, 18, 19) sts, work mouse design on next 23 sts (see graph 1 on page 92), work across rem 36 (39, 41, 42) sts. When mouse is complete, cont in color A until garment measures 10 (11, 12, 13)" from turning row of picot edging. Beg on RS row, work next rows in St st as follows:

Row 1 (RS): K1 (1, 0, 1) in color D, work graph 2 for 11 (12, 13, 13) times, end K5 (5, 4, 5) sts in color D.

Row 2 (WS): P5 (5, 4, 5) in color D, work graph 2 for 11 (12, 13, 13) times, end P1 (1, 0, 1) in color D.

Row 3: Rep row 1.

Rows 4–7: Color B, St st.

Row 8: Color C, K1, P1 across row. (Note: This row is not St st.)

Row 9: Color C, knit.

Row 10: Color A, purl.

Cont until back measures 11½ (12½, 13½, 14½)" from turning row. Beg neck and shoulder shaping.

BACK NECK AND SHOULDER SHAPING

WORK ACROSS 22 (23, 24, 25) sts, place 28 (32, 34, 34) ctr sts on st holder, join yarn, and work across rem 22 (23, 24, 25) sts. Work both shoulders for 3 rows in St st, dec 1 st at neck edge every row 2 times. BO 20 (21, 22, 23) sts for each shoulder or place on st holder for 3-needle BO.

RIGHT FRONT

PU STS from st holder and cont in color A in St st until front measures 5 (5½, 6, 6½)". Next RS row, work across 12 (14, 14, 15) sts, work cat graph on next 12 sts, beg row 1 of cat (see graph 3 on page 92), work across rem 12 (13, 14, 15) sts. Refer to page 18 for carrying yarn loosely in back. When the cat is complete, cont in St st until front measures 9 (10, 10½, 11)" from turning row. Work next 10 rows in St st as follows:

Row 1 (RS): K2 (0, 0, 2) in color D, work graph 2 for 5 (6, 6, 6) times, K4 (3, 4, 4) in color D.

Row 2 (WS): P4 (3, 4, 4) in color D, work graph 2 for 5 (6, 6, 6) times, P2 (0, 0, 2) in color D.

Row 3: Rep row 1.

Rows 4–7: Color B, St st.

Row 8: Color C, K1, P1 across row. (Note: This row is not St st.)

Row 9: Color C, knit.

Row 10: Color A, purl.

Cont until front measures 10½ (11½, 12, 12½)" from turning row. Beg neck and shoulder shaping.

FRONT NECK AND SHOULDER SHAPING

For right front: BO 12 (14, 14, 14) sts at neck edge. Work rem 24 (25, 26, 28) sts in patt, dec 1 st at neck edge EOR 4 (4, 4, 5) times. When right front measures 12 (13, 14, 15)" from turning row, BO 20 (21, 22, 23) sts for shoulder or place on st holder for 3-needle BO.

LEFT FRONT

PU sts from st holder, join yarn at inside edge, and knit across row. Work as for right front and insert cat graph 3 in color E on RS row. Cont until left front measures 9 (10, 10½, 11)" from turning row. Work next 2 rows as follows.

Row 1 (RS): K1 (0, 1, 1) in color D, work graph 2 for 5 (6, 6, 6) times, K5 (3, 3, 5) in color D.

Row 2 (WS): P5 (3, 3, 5) in color D, work graph 2 for 5 (6, 6, 6) times, P1 (0, 1, 1) in color D.

Row 3: Rep row 1.

Beg with row 3, work rem left front as for right front, reversing shaping. Join front and back shoulders.

SLEEVES

Make 2.

Sleeves are worked from the top down. They are not knit in the round, but we recommend using a circular needle. Place markers 4 (4½, 5, 5½)" from shoulder seam on front and back. With RS facing and color B, PU 50 (56, 62, 68) sts evenly between markers. Purl 1 row; knit 1 row. Work sleeve sts in alternating stripes of color A for 10 (12, 14, 16) rows and color B for 10 (12, 14, 16) rows. After completing each color A and color B stripe, work a 2-row dividing stripe in color sequence of color E, color D, color C, and color E as follows: Work RS row in K1, P1 across, work WS row in purl. For last color A stripe, work until sleeve measures 7¾ (8¾, 9¾, 10¾)". Work bottom sleeve design.

Row 1 (RS): Color B, K1, P1 across row.

Row 2 (WS): Color B, purl.

Row 3: Color D, K2, work graph 2 across row

Row 4: Work graph 2 across row, end K2 in color D.

Row 5: Color D, K2, work graph 2 across row.

Row 6: Color B, purl, dec 8 (10, 14, 16) evenly across row.

Row 7: Color C, knit.

Row 8: Purl.

Row 9: Knit.

Row 10: (Turning row) P1, *YO, P2tog, rep from * to end.

Row 11: Knit.

Row 12: Purl.

BO sts loosely.

NECK EDGING

WITH RS facing and color C, PU 82 (86, 92, 98) sts. Work in picot edging.

Rows 1, 3, and 5 (WS): Purl.

Rows 2 and 6 (RS): Knit.

Row 4 (RS): (Turning row) K2, *YO, K2tog, rep from * to end.

Row 7: Purl.

BO sts loosely.

FINISHING

SEW SIDE seams and sleeve seams together. Fold the rows worked after the turning row to the WS to finish the picot edging on sleeves and neckband. Lay the folded section flat against the garment and sew down. For bottom hem, fold rows worked before the turning row to WS and sew down.

BUTTON BAND

THIS CARDIGAN is appropriate for both boys and girls. To make this garment gender specific, buttonholes for a girl should be on the right side and buttonholes for a boy should be on the left side. Refer to "Buttonholes" on page 13. The foll instruction can be used on either side. Garment as shown has buttonholes on the right side. With RS of garment facing and color C, PU 68 (75, 82, 87) sts along left edge of garment. Include bottom hem edging but omit neck ribbing. Work in K1, P1 rib for 5 rows. BO loosely. Rep for right front edge, placing 5 (5, 6, 6) buttonholes evenly in third row.

DECORATIVE FINISHING

FINISH THE garment as shown or bring in your own creativity. The tails on the mouse and cats are worked as follows: Cut 3 lengths of yarn approx 15" long. Fold yarn length in half and tie knot in the middle. With knot at the top and using double strands of yarn, braid yarn to a length of approx 2½" to 3" long. Tie off to secure end and leave an end of yarn to pull through garment. Make a tail for each cat and the mouse. Lay the cat tails in position next to the base of the cats and pull end of yarn through to WS. Tie off tightly. Secure the top end with a needle and some yarn or thread. Make eyes with color B by pulling a single st from WS of garment to RS and back through again. Rep for cats' noses with color D. However, instead of this single st for the eyes, you can also make a French knot or purchase plastic eyes or buttons. Use ribbon or yarn to make bows for the cats.

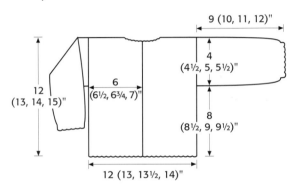

HINT: You can add a duplicate stitch to any garment after you complete the knitting and blocking. The cat's feet were done this way. A duplicate stitch covers a knit stitch with a different color of yarn. Work as follows:

1. Thread a yarn needle with the new color and bring the needle up (from the wrong side of the garment) below the stitch to be worked at the point where it makes a V.

2. Insert the needle horizontally under both loops one row above and pull it through.

3. Take the needle back into the stitch below and slide it horizontally through the center of the next stitch.

4. Repeat steps 2 and 3 as needed for desired design.

Cat Tales, Graph 1

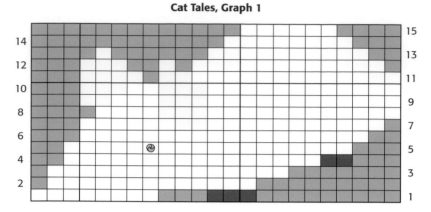

Work 23 sts x 15 row design in St st.
🌀 Button or French knot for eye

Cat Tales, Graph 2

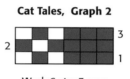

Work 6 st x 3 row
design in St st.

Cat Tales, Graph 3

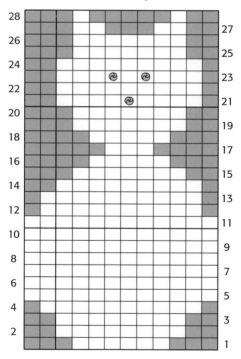

Work 12 sts x 28 row design in St st. On
right front work cat in yellow. On left front
work cat in white. If desired, add paws at
bottom of design with duplicate stitches
in a contrasting color.
🌀 Button or French knot for eyes and nose

Merry-Go-Round Pullover

$\mathcal{E}$aster parades, trips to the zoo, family reunions, and summer carnivals—this pullover would be fun to wear for any of these outings! The asymmetrical pullover is sure to be a hit. And the decorative button can be changed on a whim for a new look for any occasion.

This pattern is sized 2T (4T, 6).

•

FINISHED MEASUREMENTS

Chest: 26 (28, 30)"
Length: 12 (14, 15)"
Drop Sleeve: 10 (12, 14)"

MATERIALS

- Skacel Polo, 50-gram skeins (153 yds), 60% cotton, 40% acrylic

Color A: 51 Yellow	1 (1, 2) skeins
Color B: 54 Blue	3 (3, 4) skeins
Color C: 52 Pink	1 (1, 2) skein
Color D: 50 Green	1 (1, 1) skein

- Size 7 circular needle (24")
- Stitch holders
- Yarn needle
- 1 decorative cat button, 1" diameter

GAUGE

20 STITCHES and 28 rows = 4" in pattern stitch. To save time, always check your gauge. If necessary, change needle size to obtain correct gauge.

BODY

THIS PULLOVER is not knit in the round, but we recommend using a circular needle and working the garment in one long piece to armholes. With color A, CO 144 (154, 164) sts. Work picot edging.

Rows 1, 3, 7, and 9 (RS): Knit.

Rows 2, 4, 6, and 8 (WS): Purl.

Row 5 (RS): (Turning row) *K2tog, YO, rep from * across.

Row 10: Purl.

Cont in St st, work 2 rows in color C. Beg border design (see graph on page 95). Note, cont to work the first 2 and last 2 sts of every row in color C for rem of front until neck shaping. When border design is complete, cont in St st, 2 rows in color C, 2 rows in color A. Beg pullover body patt.

Row 1 (WS): Color B, purl.

Row 2 (RS): Color B, knit.

Row 3: Color B, purl.

Row 4: K2 in color B, *K1 in color C, K4 in color B, rep from * across.

Row 5: Color B, purl.

Row 6: Color B, knit.

Row 7: Color B, purl.

Row 8: Color B, K4, *P2, K2, rep from * across.

Rep these 8 rows until garment measures 8 (8½, 9)" from fold line in picot edging. Divide sts for back and fronts. Work across right front 52 (52, 55) sts, place back 60 (65, 70) sts on st holder, join yarn, and work across left front 32 (37, 39) sts. Work both fronts in patt until fronts measure 10 (11½, 12)". Beg front neck and shoulder shaping.

FRONT NECK AND SHOULDER SHAPING

Right front neckline: BO 30 (30, 32) sts at neck edge. Cont in patt across 22 (22, 23) sts, dec 1 st at neck edge every row 5 times. When front measures 12 (14, 15)", BO 17 (17, 18) sts for shoulder or place on st holder for 3-needle BO.

Left front neckline: BO 10 (15, 16) sts at neck edge. Cont in patt across 22 (22, 23), dec 1 st at neck edge every row 5 times. BO 17 (17, 18) sts for shoulder or place on st holder for 3-needle BO.

BACK

PU BACK sts from st holder. Work back as for front, omitting front neck shaping, until back measures 12 (14, 15)". BO 17 (17, 18) sts for each shoulder or place sts on st holder for 3-needle BO, and place ctr 26 (31, 34) sts on st holder. Join front and back shoulders.

SLEEVES

Make 2.
Sleeves are knit from the top down. They are not knit in the round, but we recommend using a circular needle. With RS facing and color A, PU 40 (45, 50) sts evenly around opening. Work sleeve in St st in the foll stripe patt:

Color B: 4 (5, 6) rows.
Color A: 3 rows.
Color C: 2 rows.
Color D: 2 (3, 4) rows.
Color C: 2 rows.
Color A: 3 rows.

Rep these rows until sleeve measures 9¾ (11¾, 13¾)". On next row, dec 10 (12, 14) sts evenly across row. With color A, work picot edge cuff as follows:

Rows 1–4: St st.
Row 5: (Turning row) *K2tog, YO, rep from * across.
Rows 6–10: St st.
BO cuff.

PICOT FRONT AND NECK EDGING

BEG AT bottom edge of right front, with RS facing and color A, PU 170 (190, 200) sts up right front, along neck edge, including sts on st holder, and down left front. Work rows 1–4 in St st. Row 5: (Turning row) *K2tog, YO, rep from * across. Work rows 6–10 in St st. BO.

FINISHING

SEW SLEEVE seams together. Fold over picot edging at fold line and stitch down with tapestry yarn needle and color A. Lightly block pullover. Lay right front over left front and secure decorative button in place.

NOTE: *The sweater is meant to slip over the child's head; no buttonhole is needed.*

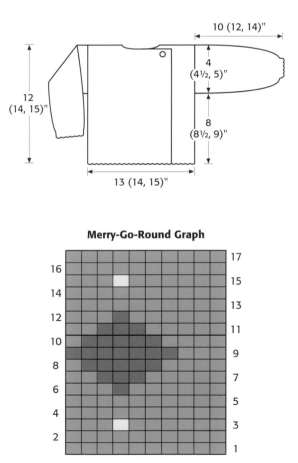

Merry-Go-Round Graph

Work 10 st x 17 row design in St st.

"Gentlemen, Start Your Engines" Cardigan

𝒯he race is on! Designed with a heavy-weight cotton yarn and big needles for a fast project, this sporty-looking cardigan is sure to be a winner with the young man who wears it.

This pattern is sized 2T (4T, 6).

●

FINISHED MEASUREMENTS

Chest: 26 (28, 30)"
Length: 13 (14, 15)"
Drop Sleeve: 10 (12, 14)"

MATERIALS

- Tahki Cotton Classic II, 50-gram skeins (74 yds), 100% cotton

  Color A: 2997 Red   1 (1, 1) skein
  Color B: 2001 White   2 (2, 3) skeins
  Color C: 2002 Black   3 (4, 4) skeins

- Size 8 circular needle (24")
- Stitch holders
- Yarn needle
- 4 or 5 black-and-white buttons, ⅝" diameter

GAUGE

18 stitches and 24 rows = 4" in pattern stitch. To save time, always check your gauge. If necessary, change needle size to obtain correct gauge.

BODY

This cardigan is not knit in the round, but we recommend using a circular needle and working the garment in one long piece to armholes. With color A, CO 114 (122, 130) sts. Work 3 rows in seed st (see page 20). Work 5 rows in St st beg with purl row. Beg 6-row checkerboard patt.

Row 1 (RS): *K2 in color B, K2 in color C, rep from * across, ending K2 color B.

Row 2 (WS): *P2 in color B, P2 in color C, rep from * across.

Row 3: *K2 in color C, K2 in color B, rep from * across, ending K2 color C.

Row 4: *P2 in color C, P2 in color B, rep from * across.

Rows 5 and 6: Rep rows 1 and 2.

Row 7: Color A, knit.

Row 8: Color A, purl.

Row 9: Color B, knit.

Row 10: Color A, purl.

Switch to color B and beg sweater patt:
(RS) rows: Knit
(WS) rows: *K1, P1, rep from * across.
Cont in seed st until cardigan measures 9 (9, 9½)". Divide sts for back and fronts. Place back 60 (64, 68) sts on st holder. Join second ball of yarn and work front 27 (29, 31) sts on each side in patt until fronts measure 11 (11½, 12½)". Beg front neck and shoulder shaping.

FRONT NECK AND SHOULDER SHAPING

BO 4 (5, 6) sts, cont in patt across rem 23 (24, 25) sts. Work both shoulders in patt, dec 1 st at neck edge every row 5 times. When front measures 13 (14, 15)", BO 18 (19, 20) sts for each shoulder or place on st holder for 3-needle BO.

BACK

PU STS from st holder and work as for front, omitting the neck shaping, until back measures 13 (14, 15)". BO 18 (19, 20) sts for each shoulder or place on st holder for 3-needle BO, and place ctr 24 (26, 28) sts on st holder. Join front and back shoulders.

SLEEVES

Make 2.
Sleeves are knit from the top down. They are not knit in the round but we recommend using a circular needle. With RS facing and color A, PU 38 (46, 50) sts evenly around opening. Work sleeve in St st in an alternating black and white 8-row stripe patt; work 6 (8, 9) stripes. Dec 1 st each edge, at end of each of last 4 stripes. In color A, work 6 rows of seed st for cuff, dec 1 st each edge on first row of cuff. BO cuff.

BUTTON BAND

WITH RS facing and color A, PU 50 (52, 56) sts. Right front: Work 2 rows of seed st. On next row, make 4 or 5 buttonholes evenly spaced down placket. See "Buttonholes" on page 13. Work 2 more rows of seed st and BO. Left front: Work 5 rows of seed st. BO.

NECK EDGING

WITH RS facing and color A, beg at right edge of right placket and PU 58 (66, 70) sts around neck opening, including sts on st holder. Work 4 rows of seed st. BO.

FINISHING

SEW SLEEVE seams together. Sew buttons with color A onto left placket. Block cardigan carefully.

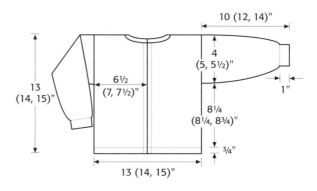

Cranberry Fizz Coatdress

$\mathcal{T}$he beautiful cherub who wears this wonderful coatdress will be ready for some holiday cheer. Knit in a hand-dyed yarn from Wool in the Woods, the garment is both a showstopper and so much fun to make! So get your camera ready. You won't want to miss an opportunity to record the littlest hit of the holiday parties decked out in this special outfit.

This pattern is sized 2T (3T, 4T).

•

FINISHED MEASUREMENTS

Chest: 24 (25, 26)"
Length: 13 (15, 17)"
Drop Sleeve: 10 (11, 12)"

MATERIALS

- Wool in the Woods Scarlet, (200 yds),
  60% mohair, 22% wool, 16% silk, 2% nylon

  Color A: Gem Jubilee   1 (2, 2) skeins
  Color B: Raspberry Fizz   2 (3, 3) skeins

- Size 8 circular needle (24")
- Stitch holders
- Yarn needle
- 2 silver buttons, ½" diameter (garment
  buttons shown are by JHB)

GAUGE

18 STITCHES and 22 rows = 4" in pattern stitch. To
save time, always check your gauge. If necessary,
change needle size to obtain correct gauge.

BODY

THIS SWEATER is not knit in the round, but we
recommend using a circular needle and working
the garment in one piece to armholes. With color
A, CO 192 (200, 208) sts. Work 8 rows of seed st.
Switch to color B and cont in seed st until garment
measures 9 (10, 11)". K2tog across next row to
shape waist. Divide sts for back and fronts. Place
back 50 (52, 54) sts on st holder. Join yarn and
work each front 23 (24, 25) sts in seed st until front
measures 11 (13, 15)". Beg front neck and shoulder
shaping.

FRONT NECK AND
SHOULDER SHAPING

WITH RS facing, BO 7 sts at each edge of neck.
Work both shoulders in seed st, dec 1 st at neck
edge every row 3 times. When front measures 13
(15, 17)", BO 13 (14, 15) sts for each shoulder or
place on st holder for 3-needle BO.

BACK

PU STS from st holder and work as for front,
omitting front neck shaping, until back measures
13 (15, 17)". BO 13 (14, 15) sts for each shoulder
or place on st holder for 3-needle BO, and place ctr
24 sts on holder. Join front and back shoulders.

SLEEVES

Make 2.
Sleeves are knit from the top down. They are not
knit in the round, but we recommend using a
circular needle. With RS facing and color C, PU 40
(44, 48) sts evenly around opening. Work in seed st
until sleeve measures 9 (10, 11)". On next row, dec
10 (12, 16) sts evenly across row. Switch to color A
and work 2" of seed st. BO cuff and fold over.

FRONT BANDS

CREATE A left and right front band. For each: With RS facing and color A, PU 44 (52, 60) sts. Right front: Work 2 rows of seed st. On the next row, create 2 buttonholes in bodice. Work 2 more rows of seed st and BO. Left front: Work 5 rows of seed st. BO.

COLLAR

WITH WS facing and color A, start at right edge of right placket and PU 54 (56, 56) sts around neck opening, including those sts on st holders. Work back and forth on the needle in St st for 4 rows. Next row, create ruffle by inc 2 in each st. Work 6 rows of K4, P4 rib. BO in K4, P4.

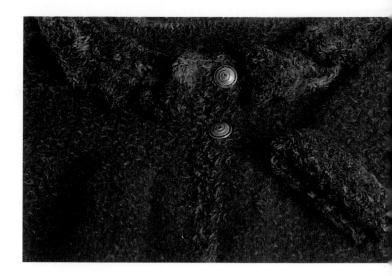

FINISHING

SEW SLEEVE seams together. Sew buttons to left placket. Block garment lightly.

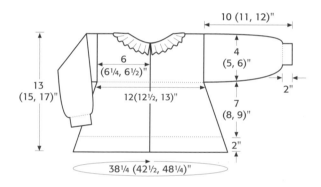

Slip, Slide, and Twist Cardigan with Hat

𝒯his yarn is so yummy. When it is time to wrap young ones up, keep them warm, and make sure they look great, this cardigan and hat will be a perfect choice. We combined cable and slip stitch to make an interesting, textured, stylish outfit that will take your snow bunny from the grocery store to Gucci's.

Cardigan

This pattern is sized 2T (4T, 6).

•

FINISHED MEASUREMENTS

Chest: 26 (30, 34)"
Length: 13 (15, 17)"
Sleeve: 10 (12, 14)"

MATERIALS

- Cascade Yarns Pastaza, 100-gram skeins (132 yds), 50% llama, 50% wool

Color A: 6002 Blue	4 (5, 6) skeins
Color B: 6003 Poppy	1 (1, 1) skein
Color C: 052 Green	1 (1, 1) skein
Color D: 026 Taupe	1 (1, 1) skein

- Size 10 circular needle (24")
- Size 10½ circular needle (24")
- Stitch holders
- Yarn needle
- 5 (6, 6) buttons, ¾" diameter

GAUGE

17 STITCHES and 28 rows = 4" in two-by-two check pattern on size 10½ needle.

22 stitches and 27 rows = 4" in two-color cable rib pattern on size 10 needle.

To save time, always check your gauge. If necessary, change needle size to obtain correct gauge.

BOTTOM BORDER

THIS CARDIGAN is not knit in the round, but we recommend using a circular needle and working the garment in one piece to armholes. With size 10 needle and color D, CO 120 (136, 156) sts.

Switch to color A, work K2, P2 rib for 3 rows. Switch to size 10½ needle, beg two-by-two check patt for bottom border. This patt has an 8-row rep, at which point the colors for B, C, and D change positions. Work as follows for color sequence 1 (color sequences 2 and 3 are in parentheses).

Row 1 (RS): Color B (C, D), *K2, sl 2 wyib; rep from * to end. Do not turn work; slide sts to other end of needle.

Row 2 (RS): Color A, *sl 2 wyib, K2; rep from * to end. Turn work.

Row 3 (WS): Color C (D, B), *sl 2 wyif, P2; rep from * to end. Do not turn work; slide sts to other end of needle.

Row 4 (WS): Color A, *P2, sl 2 wyif; rep from * to end. Turn work.

Row 5 (RS): Color D (B, C), *sl 2 wyib, K2; rep from * to end. Do not turn work; slide sts to other end of needle.

Row 6 (RS): Color A, *K2, sl 2 wyib, rep from * to end. Turn work.

Row 7 (WS): Color B (C, D), *P2, sl 2 wyif, rep from * to end. Do not turn work; slide sts to other end of needle.

Row 8 (WS): Color A, *sl 2 wyif, P2; rep from * to end. Turn work.

Size 2T: Rep rows 1–8, work color sequences 2, 3, then rows 1–4 of color sequence 1—total 28 rows.

Sizes 4T and 6: Rep rows 1–8, work color sequences 2, 3, then 8 rows of color sequence 1—total 32 rows.

Next row (RS): Switch to size 10 needle, and with color A, knit across, inc 20 (28, 32) sts evenly across row.

With color D, purl 1 row; then knit 1 row—140 (164, 188) sts.

BODY

Work remainder of cardigan body in two-color cable rib, working 1 selvage st in St st on each side of patt row. The cable patt can leave an uneven edge to PU button band sts. An extra st at each edge enables a smoother PU and does not distort the cable patt. This patt has a 6-row rep with rows 1 and 2 changing color with each rep. Work as follows for color sequence 1 (color sequences 2 and 3 are in parentheses).

Row 1 (WS): Color B (C, D), P1 (selvage st), K2, *P6, K2; rep from * to end, P1 (selvage st).

Row 2 (RS): Color B (C, D), K1 (selvage st), P2, *sl 1 wyib, K4, sl 1 wyib, P2; rep from * to end, K1 (selvage st).

Row 3 (WS): Color A, P1, K2, *sl 1 wyif, P4, sl 1 wyif, K2; rep from * to end, P1.

Row 4 (RS): Color A, K1, P2, *sl 1 wyib, K4, sl 1 wyib, P2; rep from* to end, K1.

Row 5 (WS): Color A, P1, K2, *sl 1 wyif, P4, sl 1 wyif, K2; rep from * to end, P1.

Row 6 (RS): Color A, K1, P2, *drop slip st off needle to front of work (it will lie on the surface of the garment), K2; then PU slip st and knit it (do not twist st), sl next 2 sts to RH needle, drop next slip st off needle to front of work, then sl the 2 sts back on the LH needle, PU dropped st with right needle, replace it on left needle and knit it, K2, P2, rep from * to end, K1.

Rep rows 1–6, working color sequences 2, 3, and starting again with 1 until garment measures 8½ (10, 11½)" from beg, ending on WS row. Divide sts for back and fronts. Mark patt so that each section will be cont at point of division. On RS, work 34 (42, 46) sts in patt and place on st holder for right front, work across 72 (80, 96) sts, place rem 34 (42, 46) sts on st holder for left front.

BACK

Cont in patt until garment measures 12½ (14½, 16½)", assess if patt can be completed in the next 3 rows. If so, complete patt. If not, work row 1 in color A if WS row; if RS row, P2, *K6, P2, rep from *. If it takes more than these 2 rows to reach 13 (15, 17)", stay in patt as written. Work across 19 (21, 25) sts and place on st holder for 3-needle BO, BO 34 (38, 46) ctr sts, join yarn and work across rem 19 (21, 25) sts and place on st holder.

LEFT FRONT

Left front was placed on st holder without having last RS row worked as on right front and back. Beg on the RS, attach yarn at inside edge of left front section and cont in patt until left front measures 12 (13½, 15½)". At neck edge, BO 10 (13, 13) sts and work in patt across row. Cont in patt, dec 1 st at neck edge every row 5 (8, 8) times. When left front measures 13 (15, 17)", place 19 (21, 25) sts on st holder for 3-needle BO.

RIGHT FRONT

With WS facing, attach yarn at inside edge of right front section. Work in patt as for left front, reversing neck and shoulder shaping. Join front and back shoulders.

SLEEVES

Make 2.

Sleeves are worked from the top down. They are not worked in the round, but we recommend using a circular needle. With RS facing, size 10 needle, and color A, PU 40 (46, 52) sts evenly around opening. Work in St st for 2". Next row, dec 4 (6, 8) sts evenly across row. Cont in St st until sleeve measures 8 (10, 12)", ending on WS row. Next row, dec 4 sts evenly across row. Work cuff on rem 32 (36, 40) sts as follows:

Row 1 (WS): Color D, purl.

Rows 2–9: Switch to size 10½ needle, work 8 rows of two-by-two check patt, ending on WS row.

Row 10 (RS): Switch to size 10 needle, color A, knit.

Row 11: Color A, *K2, P2, rep from * across row.

Row 12: Color A, *P2, K2, rep from * across row.

Row 13: In color D, rep row 11.

BO sts in patt.

BUTTON BAND

With RS facing and color C, PU 44 (50, 56) sts along left front edge of sweater.

Row 1: *K2, P2, rep from * across row.

Row 2: Knit the purl sts and purl the knit sts.

Rep rows 1 and 2 until 7 (5, 5) rows have been worked. BO in patt st.

Rep for right front edge, working 5 (6, 6) buttonholes in 4th (3rd, 3rd) row of button band. Refer to "Buttonholes" on page 13.

COLLAR

With RS of garment facing, size 10 needle, and color B, PU 54 (62, 70) sts around neck edge. Do not PU sts across button band, but do beg at the inside edge. Work as follows until collar measures 2 (2½, 3)".

Row 1 (WS): *K2, P2, rep from * across row.

Row 2 (RS): Knit the purl sts and purl the knit sts.

Rep rows 1 and 2 until collar is 2 (2½, 3)".

BO in patt st.

FINISHING

Sew sleeve seams together. Sew buttons on button band to correspond with buttonholes. Block garment lightly.

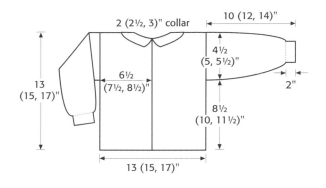

Hat

This pattern is sized Small (Medium, Large).

•

FINISHED MEASUREMENTS

Circumference: 16 (18, 20)"

MATERIALS

- Cascade Yarns Pastaza, 100-gram skeins (132 yds), 50% llama, 50% wool. In some cases, the remnant yarn from the cardigan will be sufficient to make the hat. If this hat is being worked independently, use 1 skein of each of the foll colors:

  Color A: 6002 Blue
  Color B: 6003 Poppy
  Color C: 052 Green
  Color D: 026 Taupe

- Size 10 circular needle (24")
- Size 10½ circular needle (24")
- Yarn needle

GAUGE

17 STITCHES and 28 rows = 4" in two-by-two check pattern on size 10½ needle.

BAND

THIS HAT is not knit in the round, but we recommend using a circular needle. With size 10 needle and color D, CO 68 (76, 84) sts.

(WS): Color A, work 3 rows in K2, P2 rib.

(RS): Switch to size 10½ needle, work 12 (16, 20) rows of two-by-two check patt as for bottom border of sweater (see page 103).

(RS): Color D, switch to size 10 needle, work 3 rows in St st, dec 2 sts in last row.

(WS): Work 6 rows of two-color cable rib patt as for sweater body (see page 104).

(WS): Color B, knit 1 row.

(RS): K2, P2 across all sts for 7 (9, 11) rows.

(WS): Color A, knit 1 row.

(RS): Work remainder of hat in St st to completion. With color C, work 2 rows. For medium size, dec 2 sts in last row; for large size, inc 2 sts in last row for crown shaping.

CROWN

(RS): *K2tog, K9 (10, 10) sts, place marker; rep from * across row 5 times more—6 sts dec.

(WS): Purl 1 row.

(RS): *K2tog, K8 (9, 9) sts; rep from * across row 5 times more—6 sts dec.

(WS): Purl 1 row.

(RS): Cont to K2tog and work the dec progression of 8, 7, 6, 5, 4 sts in each RS row until 6 sts rem. Cut long tail of yarn (enough to use for back seam) and pull through sts.

FINISHING

USING YARN end from crown sts, sew back seam of hat together.

TASSEL

USING 4 yarn colors in hat, wrap yarn 50 times around a 3" index card or any object of similar size. Cut a length of yarn and slip through wrapped yarn. Tie tightly and slip tassel off card. Holding tassel securely by one end, cut loops open at opposite end. Secure tassel through ctr of top. Tie off tightly in WS of hat. Trim to desired length.

16 (18, 20)"

Trim the Tree Pullover

Deck those halls, jingle those bells—and get the children you know ready for the holidays. Whether they're off to a holiday party or a Christmas dinner with family, a boy or a girl would look terrific in this festive pullover.

This pattern is sized 2T (4T, 6, 8, 10).

●

FINISHED MEASUREMENTS

Chest: 26 (28, 30, 32, 34)"
Length: 12 (14, 15, 16, 17)"
Drop Sleeve: 10 (11¼, 12¼, 14, 15¼)"

MATERIALS

- Dale of Norway Freestyle, 50-gram skeins (75 yds), 100% wool

Color A: 4018 Red	4 (5, 6, 6, 7) skeins
Color B: 7073 Green	2 (2, 2, 2, 3) skeins
Color C: 0010 White	1 (1, 1, 1, 1) skein

- Size 7 straight needles (for fun try Z'Needlz by Zecca)
- Size 7 circular needle (24") for sleeves and neck
- Stitch holders
- Tapestry needle
- Assortment of Christmas buttons, ½" to 1¼" diameter (garment buttons shown are by Mill Hill, JHB)
- 3 small red buttons for snowflake centers, ⅜" diameter

GAUGE

20 STITCHES and 24 rows = 4" in pattern stitch. To save time, always check your gauge. If necessary, change needle size to obtain correct gauge.

BABY CABLE RIBBING

Rows 1 and 3 (WS): K2, *P2, K2, rep from * across.

Row 2 (RS): P2, *K2, P2, rep from * across.

Row 4: P2, *K2 tog but leave on needle, then insert right needle between the 2 sts just knitted tog and knit the first again, then sl both sts from needle tog, P2, rep from * across.

Rep rows 1–4.

FRONT

THIS PULLOVER is not knit in the round, but we recommend using a circular needle. With color A, CO 66 (70, 76, 80, 86) sts. Work 11 rows in baby cable ribbing (all sizes). Beg patt for pullover body.

Rows 1, 5, 7, and 9 (RS): Color A, knit.

Rows 2, 4, 6, and 8 (WS): Color A, purl.

Row 3 (RS): K4 in color A, *K1 in color C, K9 in color A, rep from * across, end K4 in color A.

Row 10 (WS): *P10 in color A, P1 in color C, rep from * across.

Rep rows 1–10 until front measures 2½ (3, 3½, 4, 4½)", beg tree (see graph 1 on page 110). Work 10 (12, 15, 17, 20) sts in patt, work graph 1 in St st, work last 11 (13, 16, 18, 21) sts in patt. When tree is complete, cont in patt until front measures 10 (11½, 12, 13, 13½)". Beg front neck and shoulder shaping.

FRONT NECK AND SHOULDER SHAPING

WITH RS facing, work across 23 (24, 26, 27, 28) sts. Place ctr 20 (22, 24, 26, 30) sts on st holder. Join second ball of yarn and work across rem 23

(24, 26, 27, 28) sts. Work both shoulders in St st, dec 1 st at neck edge every row 5 times. When front measures 12 (14, 15, 16, 17)", BO 18 (19, 21, 22, 23) sts for each shoulder or place on st holder for 3-needle BO.

BACK

CO 66 (70, 76, 80, 86) sts. Work as for front, omitting tree design and front neck shaping, until garment measures 8 (9½, 10, 10½, 11)". On next RS row, change to color B and knit next 2 rows. Next row, purl. Switch to color A, resume St st as you beg yoke snowflake design (see graph 2 on page 110). Place 3 snowflakes evenly across back of sweater as follows: Work 6 (7, 8, 9, 11) sts, work graph 2, work 7 (8, 10, 11, 12) sts, work graph 2, work 7 (8, 10, 11, 12) sts, work graph 2, work last 7 (8, 9, 10, 12) sts. After snowflakes are complete, work in St st until back measures 11¾ (13¾, 14¾, 15¾, 16¾)". Next row, knit 2 rows in color B. BO 18 (19, 21, 22, 23) sts for each shoulder or place on st holder for 3-needle BO, and place ctr 30 (32, 34, 36, 40) sts on holder. Join front and back shoulders.

SLEEVES

Make 2.

Sleeves are knit from the top down. They are not knit in the round, but we recommend using a circular needle. Place markers 4 (4½, 5, 5½, 6)" from shoulder seam on front and back. With RS facing and color A, PU 38 (46, 50, 54, 58) sts evenly

between markers. Work in St st in an 8-row stripe patt of colors A and B, complete 6 (7, 8, 9, 10) stripes. Work cuff as follows: Sizes 2T (6, 8): Work 2 rows of color A in St st. All sizes: Work 6 rows of checkerboard in St st as follows:

Row 1: *K2 in color B, K2 in color C, rep from * across, ending K2 color B.
Row 2: *P2 in color B, P2 in color C, rep from * across.
Row 3: *K2 in color C, K2 in color B, rep from * across, ending color C.
Row 4: *P2 in color C, P2 in color B, rep from * across.
Rows 5 and 6: Rep rows 1 and 2.
Next row: In color B, dec 10 (11, 12, 13, 14) sts evenly across row.

Work the next 4 rows in St st. BO cuff, letting it roll back slightly.

NECK EDGING

With RS facing, beg at one shoulder seam in color B and PU 68 (76, 84, 92, 100) sts around neck opening, including those sts on st holders. Place marker to designate beg of rnd, and join ends. Knit 6 rnds. BO loosely, letting neck edge roll over.

FINISHNG

Sᴇw sʟᴇᴇᴠᴇ and side seams together. Block garment lightly. Secure buttons to the Christmas tree as desired by tying them from behind with colors A, B, or C. Secure small red button in center of each snowflake with French knot in color C.

Trim the Tree, Graph 2

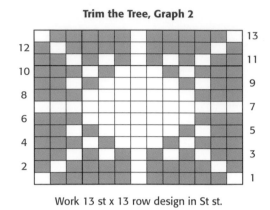

Work 13 st x 13 row design in St st.

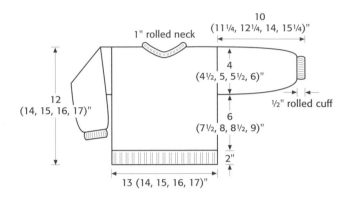

Trim the Tree, Graph 1

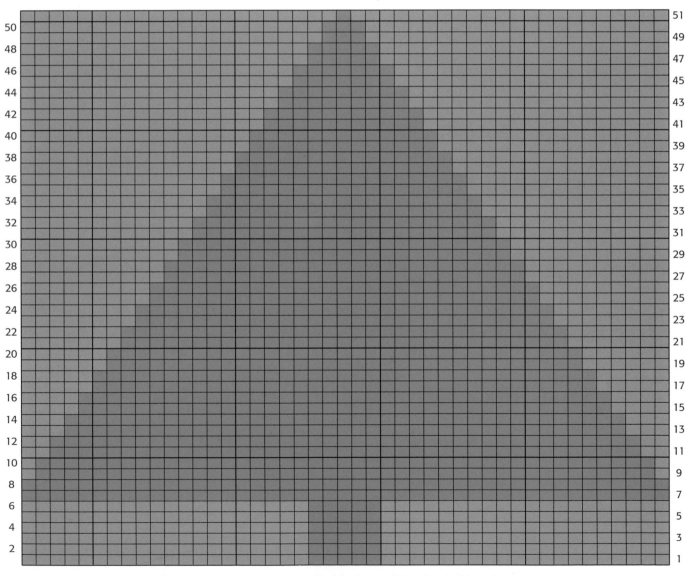

Work 45 st x 51 row design in St st. Work background in red and white pattern as est.

Skating Party Jacket with Hat

On a cold winter's night, this velvety soft jacket and hat will keep a precious girl warm and cozy as she skates figure eights on the ice.

Jacket

This pattern is sized 2T (3T, 4T).

•

FINISHED MEASUREMENTS

Chest: 26 (27, 28)"
Length: 13 (14, 15)"
Drop Sleeve: 10 (11, 12)"

MATERIALS

- Wendy Velvet Touch from Berroco, Inc., 50-gram skeins (114 yds), 100% nylon

  Color A: 1202 Red   7 (7, 8) skeins
  Color B: 2007 Black   1 (1, 1) skein

- Size 7 circular needle (24")
- Stitch holders
- Medium-sized crochet hook
- Sewing needle and red thread
- Yarn needle

GAUGE

16 STITCHES and 24 rows = 4" in pattern stitch. To save time, always check your gauge. If necessary, change needle size to obtain correct gauge.

BODY

THIS SWEATER is not knit in the round, but we recommend using a circular needle and working this garment in one piece to armholes. With color

A, CO 156 (162, 168) sts. Work 2 rows in seed st (see page 00). Cont in St st until garment measures 3 (3½, 4)". On next RS row, *K2tog, K1, rep from * across—104 (108, 112) sts. Cont in St st until garment measures 9 (9½, 10)". Divide sts for back and 2 fronts. Place back 52 (54, 56) sts on st holder. Join second ball of yarn and cont in St st on 26 (27, 28) sts for each front until fronts measure 11 (11½, 12½)". Beg front neck and shoulder shaping.

FRONT NECK AND SHOULDER SHAPING

BO 6 sts at neck edge. Cont in St st across rem 20 (21, 22) sts. Work both shoulders at same time, dec 1 st at neck edge every row 6 times. When front measures 13 (14, 15)", BO 14 (15, 16) sts for each shoulder or place on st holder for 3-needle BO.

BACK

PU BACK sts from st holder. Work as for front, omitting front neck shaping. When back measures 13 (14, 15)", BO 14 (15, 16) sts for each shoulder or place on st holder for 3-needle BO, and place ctr 24 sts on st holder. Join front and back shoulders.

SLEEVES

Make 2.
Sleeves are knit from the top down. They are not knit in the round, but we recommend using a circular needle. With RS facing and color A, PU 40 (42, 44) sts evenly around opening. Work in St st until sleeve measures 9 (10, 11)". On next row, dec 10 sts evenly across row. With color B, work 1" of seed st for cuff. BO.

COLLAR

WITH WS facing and color B, beg at edge of left placket and PU 52 (56, 56) sts around neck opening, including sts on st holder. Work 14 rows of seed st. BO.

FRONT BANDS

WITH RS facing and color A, PU 44 (46, 50) sts along left front. Work 6 rows of St st. BO. Rep for right front.

FINISHING

SEW SLEEVE seams together. To make ties: With color B, make 2 crochet chains (see page 20), 10" to 12" long. Make 2 small pom-poms by winding several yards of color B around a 2"-wide piece of cardboard. Slide off and tie in the middle securely, leaving long tail from the tie to secure to one end of each crochet chain. Trim and fluff pom-poms. Fold front plackets back. Secure other end of each chain behind the fold of placket 1½" from neck edge. Tack down with sewing needle and thread.

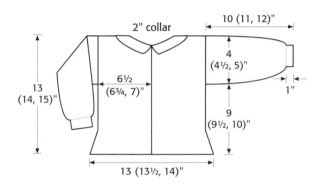

Hat

This pattern is sized Small (Medium, Large).

•

FINISHED MEASUREMENTS

Circumference: 16 (18, 20)"

MATERIALS

- Wendy Velvet Touch from Berroco, Inc., 50-gram skeins (114 yds), 100% nylon

  Color A: 1202 Red   2 (2, 2) skeins
  Color B: 2007 Black   1 (1, 1) skein

- Size 8 circular needle (16")
- Medium-sized crochet hook
- Stitch markers
- Yarn needle

GAUGE

16 STITCHES and 20 rows = 4" in pattern stitch.

BRIM

THIS HAT is knit using 2 strands of yarn. It is not knit in the round, but we recommend using a circular needle. With color A, CO 12 sts (all sizes). Work in St st until strip measures 16 (18, 20)". Join ends together to form circle. PU 64 (72, 80) sts along edge of brim. Place marker to designate beg of rnd. Place st markers every 16 (18, 20) sts. Work as follows:

Rnd 1: Knit.
Rnd 2: *Knit to marker, K2tog, rep from * around.

Rep rnds 1 and 2 for a total of 18 (20, 24) rnds.

Next rnd: *Knit to 2 sts before marker, K2tog, move marker to right needle, K2tog, rep from * around.

Rep last rnd. BO rem sts. Tie together tightly.

FINISHING

WITH A single strand of color B, single crochet around bottom edge of hat and around brim of hat as shown in photo on page 111. To make tassel with color B, crochet 4 chains 6" long (see page 20). Secure 1 chain to each of the 4 corners on crown. Tie chains together at crown of hat.

16 (18, 20)"

Fuzzy Wuzzy Pullover with Pants and Hat

$\mathcal{T}$his is one of those outfits that once you put it on a youngster, you will never get it off! We designed it to be comfortable in every way—generous proportions, easy access, and in a favorite color combination of red, white, and blue. Don't be surprised if your favorite "fuzzy wuzzy" insists on sleeping in this one.

Pullover

The pullover and pant patterns
are sized 18M (2T, 3T, 4T).

•

FINISHED MEASUREMENTS

Chest: 24 (26, 28, 30)"
Pullover Length: 11 (13, 14, 15)"
Sleeve: 9 (10, 11, 12)"
Pant Length: 17 (18½, 20, 22)"

MATERIALS

- Wendy Velvet Touch from Berroco, Inc.,
  50-gram skeins (114 yds), 100% nylon
  Yarn amounts are for pullover and pants.

  Color A: 1203 Blue   4 (4, 5, 6) skeins
  Color B: 1200 White   2 (2, 3, 3) skeins
  Color C: 1202 Red   2 (2, 2, 2) skeins

- Size 7 circular needle (24") for body
- Size 4 circular needle (24") for ribbing
- Five size 4 double-pointed needles for hat
- Stitch holders
- Tapestry needle

GAUGE

17 STITCHES and 28 rows = 4" in stockinette
stitch. To save time, always check your gauge. If nec
essary, change needle size to obtain correct gauge.

FRONT

THIS PULLOVER is not knit in the round, but we
recommend using a circular needle. With size 4
needle and color C, CO 52 (54, 58, 62) sts. Beg K2,
P2 rib.

Row 1 (WS): *P2, K2, rep from * across.

Row 2 (RS): *K2, P2, rep from * across.

Rows 3 and 4: Rep rows 1 and 2.

Row 5: Purl across row, inc 0 (2, 0,2) sts in row—
52 (56, 58, 64) sts. Place marker after 26 (28,
29, 32) sts to indicate ctr front. Left half of
the garment is worked in color C, right half
is worked in a stripe patt of color A for 8
rows and color B for 2 rows.

Switch to size 7 needle and work body of pullover
in St st in the foll color sequence:

Rows 1–10: Color B, St st beg with knit row.

Rows 11 and 12: Work 26 (28, 29, 32) sts in color
C, 26 (28, 29, 32) sts in color A.

Rows 13 and 14: Color B, St st.

Row 15: K2 (1, 2, 2) in color B, *K1 in color C, K2
in color B, rep from * across to ctr marker,
then *K2 in color B, K1 in color A, rep from
* across, end K2 (1, 2, 2) in color B.

Rows 16–19: Color B, St st.

Row 20: P2 (1, 2, 2) in color B, *P1 in color A, P2
in color B, rep from * to ctr marker, then P2
in color B, P1 in color C, rep from * across,
end P2 (1, 2, 2) in color B.

Rows 21 and 22: Color B, St st.

Rows 23 and 24: Color C, work to ctr marker,
color A, work to end of row. Stay in color
patt on return row.

Rows 25 and 26: Color B, St st. Size 3T only, in
row 26, inc 1 st on each end of needle—60 sts.

Rows 27–34: Work color C to marker, work color
A to end. This est the color patt of color C
for entire left front, and color patt for right

front in stripes of 8 rows of color A, 2 rows of color B.

Rep rows 25–34 until front measures 10 (12, 13, 13½)". Note for size 3T: Do not work additional inc in row 26. Beg front neck and shoulder shaping.

FRONT NECK AND SHOULDER SHAPING

WITH RS facing, staying in color patt, work across 17 (18, 20, 21) sts, BO 18 (20, 20, 22) ctr sts, join second ball of yarn, and work across rem 17 (18, 20, 21) sts. Work both shoulders in patt, dec 1 st at neck edge EOR 2 (2, 3, 3) times. When front measures 11 (13, 14, 15)", BO 15 (16, 17, 18) sts for each shoulder or place on st holder for 3-needle BO.

BACK

REVERSE COLOR patt and work as for front, omitting neck and shoulder shaping. As back is worked, the right side facing is in blue and the left side facing is in red. When assembled, blue front goes to blue back and red goes to red. Cont in patt until back measures 10½ (12½, 13½, 14½)". Work across 16 (17, 18, 19) shoulder sts, BO 20 (22, 24, 26) ctr sts, join second ball of yarn and work across rem 16 (17, 18, 19) sts. Work both shoulders in patt, dec 1 st at neck edge one time. When back measures 11 (13, 14, 15)", BO 15 (16, 17, 18) sts for each shoulder or place on st holder as for front. Join front and back shoulders.

SLEEVES

SLEEVES ARE knit from the top down. They are not knit in the round, but we recommend using circular needles. Place markers 4 (4½, 5, 5½)" from shoulder seam on front and back. With RS facing and color B, PU 36 (40, 44, 48) sts evenly between markers.

Right sleeve: With color B, purl return row. Cont in stripe patt as est in pullover body, work 8 rows in color A, 2 rows in color B, until sleeve measures 8½ (9½, 10½, 11½)" ending on RS row. Next row, with color B, purl, dec 6 (8, 10, 12) sts evenly across row. Switch to size 4 needle and color C, work K2, P2 rib on next 4 rows for cuff. BO loosely in patt.

Left sleeve: Work as for right sleeve except stripes, work 8 rows in color C. All color B rows rem the same. Work cuff in color A.

NECK EDGING

WITH SIZE 4 needle, RS facing, and color B, PU 64 (68, 72, 76) sts around neck edge. Place marker to designate beg of rnd, and join ends.

Rnds 1–6: Color B, *K2, P2, rep from * around.

Rnds 7–9: Color C, knit.

Rnds 10–13: Switch to size 7 needle, color C, knit.

Rnd 14: Color A, purl.

BO in purl st. Ribbing will roll forward and fold itself in half.

FINISHING

SEW SIDE seams and sleeve seams together. Hint: For left side, use color B to stitch up to the solid section, and then change to color C. For right side, use color B to stitch up to the stripe section, and then change to color A.

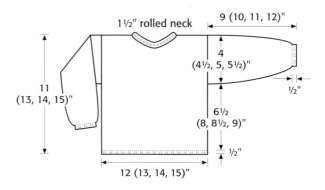

Pants

LEGS

Make 2.

With size 4 needle and color C, CO 40 (44, 48, 52) sts. Work next row in K2, P2 rib. In color B, work rib patt for 10 (12, 14, 14) rows, inc 31 (33, 35, 37) sts in last row—71 (77, 83, 89) sts. Switch to size 7 needle and work pants in St st in foll color sequence:

Color A: 8 (10, 10, 10) rows.

Color B: 2 rows.

Color A: 2 rows.

Next row: 2 sts in color A, 1 st in color B.

Color A: 4 rows.

Next row: 2 sts in color A, 1 st in color B.

Color A: 2 rows.

Color B: 2 rows.

Color A: 8 (10, 10, 10) rows.

Color B: 2 rows.

Color A: 1 row.

Color B: 1 row.

Color A: 1 row.

Color B: 2 rows.

Color A: 8 (10, 10, 10) rows.

Color B: 4 rows.

Next row: 2 sts in color B, 1 st in color A.

Color B: 4 rows.

***Color A:** 8 rows.

Color B: 2 rows, rep from * in color sequence until garment measures 10 (10½, 11½, 13)" or desired measurement from bottom of cuff. Beg crotch shaping.

CROTCH SHAPING AND BODY

WITH RS facing, work across sts for one leg to end of row, CO 3 sts, cont across sts for second leg, CO 3 sts. Place marker to designate beg of rnd, and join ends. Cont rnds in color sequence until garment measures 12 (13, 14, 15)". Next rnd, dec 22 (24, 26, 28) sts evenly in rnd. Cont until garment measures 15 (16½, 18, 20)" from beg. For waistband shaping, with size 4 needle, dec 22 (24, 26, 28) evenly in rnd. Work as follows:

Color B: Knit 1 rnd.

Color B: *K2, P2, rep from * for 1 rnd.

Color A: *K2, P2, rep from * for 8 (9, 10, 11) rnds.

Color A: Purl 1 rnd.

BO sts loosely.

I-CORD TIE

WITH SIZE 4 dpn or circular needle and color B, CO 3 sts. Do not turn. Hold yarn in back of work, pulling it behind CO sts, K3. Do not turn. *Keep working yarn in back of needle and slide sts to the other end, K3. Without turning work, rep from * until tie measures 36" to 42". Garment size and individual size will determine length. When completed, thread tail of yarn through the sts and pull tightly.

FINISHING

SEW LEG seams together. Beg ½" from ctr front and weave I-cord tie through waistband at even intervals. Use a crochet hook to help pull tie through waistband sts.

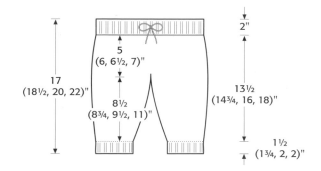

Hat

> This pattern is sized Small (Medium, Large).
>
> •
>
> FINISHED MEASUREMENTS
>
> Circumference: 16½ (18, 19½)"

MATERIALS

- Wendy Velvet Touch from Berroco, Inc., 50-gram skeins (114 yds), 100% nylon. In some cases, the remnant yarn from the pullover will be sufficient to make the hat. If this hat is being worked independently, use 1 skein of each of the foll colors:

  Color A: 1203 Blue
  Color B: 1200 White
  Color C: 1202 Red

- Size 4 circular needle (24")
- 5 size 4 double-pointed needles

GAUGE

21 STITCHES and 32 rows = 4" in stockinette stitch.

BAND

WITH SIZE 4 circular needle and color A, CO 88 (96, 104) sts. Place marker to designate beg of rnd, and join ends. With color B, *K1, P1, rep from * for 8 (10, 12) rnds. With color C, knit 2 rnds.

BODY

BEG CHECKERBOARD patt.

Rnds 1–4: *K4 in color B, K4 in color A, rep from * to marker.

Rnds 5–8: *K4 in color A, K4 in color C, rep from * to marker.

Rnds 9–12: *K4 in color C, K4 in color B, rep from * to marker.

For large size, rep rnds 1–4.

Work 4 stripes as follows:

Color A: 5 (6, 8) rnds.
Color B: 2 rnds.
Color C: 5 (6, 8) rnds.
Color B: 2 rnds.
Color A: 5 (6, 8) rnds.
Color B: 2 rnds.

CROWN

DIVIDE STS evenly onto 4 size 4 dpns. *Place 22 (24, 26) sts on needle #1, place marker, and rep for needles #2, #3, and #4. With color C, work 3 (4, 6) rnds. In rnds 4 (5, 7) (dec rnd), K2tog on each side of marker for needles #1, #2, #3, and #4— 8 sts dec. Rep dec rnd. With color B, work 1 rnd even, work 1 dec rnd as above. Work 1 rnd in color A, 1 dec rnd in color C as above. Work 1 rnd in color B, 3 rnds in color C. Cut yarn, leaving long tail to pull through rem sts. Draw up tightly to secure crown.

POM-POM

USING THE 3 garment colors, wrap yarn 50 to 60 times around a 3" index card. (A checkbook also works well!) Cut a length of yarn and slip through wrapped yarn. Tie tightly and slip pom-pom off card. Holding pom-pom securely by one end, cut loops open at opposite end. Secure pom-pom through ctr of top. Tie off tightly on WS of hat. Trim pom-pom to desired length.

16½ (18, 19½)"

Harvest Moon Cardigan with Pants

$\mathcal{A}$utumn leaves, an orange moon, chilly days, and candy corn—we were in the mood for an outfit that would close out the summer and bring in the fall when we designed this one. We worked the sweater in cotton in a slip-stitch and stockinette pattern, and we were pleased with the look and texture created by the blending of the vibrant colors.

Cardigan

This pattern is sized 18M (2T, 3T, 4T).

•

FINISHED MEASUREMENTS

Chest: 24 (26, 27, 28)"
Cardigan Length: 11 (12, 13, 14)"
Sleeves: 9 (10, 11, 12)"
Pant Length: 17 (19, 20, 22)"

MATERIALS

- Tahki Cotton Classic, 50-gram skeins
  (108 yds), 100% cotton

  Cardigan
Color A: 3407 Rust	1 (1, 1, 2) skeins
Color B: 3356 Gold	2 (2, 2, 3) skeins
Color C: 3331 Brown	1 (1, 1, 1) skein
Color D: 3609 Green	2 (2, 2, 2) skeins
Color E: 3327 Cinnamon	1 (1, 1, 1) skein

  Pants
Color A: 3407 Rust	1 (1, 1, 1) skein
Color B: 3356 Gold	1 (1, 1, 1) skein
Color C: 3331 Brown	2 (2, 3, 4) skeins
Color D: 3609 Green	2 (2, 3, 4) skeins

- Size 6 circular needle (24")
- Stitch holders
- Tapestry needle
- 5 (5, 6, 6) buttons for cardigan, ½" diameter
  (garment buttons shown are by JHB)
- 2 (3, 3, 3) buttons for pants, ½" diameter
  (garment buttons shown are by JHB)

GAUGE

Cardigan: 23 stitches and 32 rows = 4" in
   stockinette stitch.
Pants: 24 stitches and 38 rows = 4" in pattern
   stitch.
To save time, always check your gauge. If necessary,
change needle size to obtain correct gauge.

HONEYCOMB TWEED SLIP-STITCH PATTERN

Row 1 (RS): K1, *sl 1 wyib, K1, rep from *.
Row 2 (WS): Purl.
Row 3: K2, *sl 1 wyib, K1, rep from *, end K1.
Row 4: Purl.
Rep rows 1–4.

BODY

THIS CARDIGAN is not knit in the round, but we
recommend using a circular needle and working
the garment in one piece to armholes. With color
A, CO 134 (142, 150, 158) sts. For bottom border,
work P2, K2 rib for 3 rows. Change to color B and
rep rib patt and rows. Next (WS) row, purl. Beg
cardigan stripes.
Stripe 1 (RS): With color E, work St st for 2 (4, 4,
   4) rows, inc 1 st in last row. With color D,
   work 6 (8, 8, 8) rows in seed st (see page 20).
   With color E, work St st for 2 (4, 4, 4) rows.
Stripe 2: In honeycomb tweed sl st patt, work
   rows 1 and 2 in color A, rows 3 and 4 in
   color D. With color B, work 12 (14, 16, 18)
   rows in St st.

Stripe	Rows 1 and 2: Sl st patt	Rows 3 and 4: Sl st patt	12 (14, 16, 18) rows in St st
3	Color C	Color A	Color D
4	Color B	Color C	Color A
5	Color D	Color B	Color C

Rep stripe 2 for stripes 3, 4, and 5, but in the foll color sequence as indicated above.
(While working in stripe sequence, be aware of instructions for garment shaping.)
When cardigan measures 6 (6½, 7, 7½)" from beg, divide sts for back and 2 fronts. Next RS row, work in patt across 33 (35, 37, 39) sts and place on st holder for right front. Work across 68 (72, 76, 80) back sts in patt, inc 1 st in row (not at the end), place rem 33 (35, 37, 39) sts on st holder for left front.

BACK

CONT ON 69 (73, 77, 81) sts in honeycomb tweed sl st patt and color sequence as est. When you complete stripe 5, work row 1 of sl st patt in color A. Next row, purl across 23 (25, 25, 27) sts; place 23 (23, 27, 27) sts on st holder; join second ball of yarn and work across 23 (25, 25, 27) sts. For both shoulders, with color D, work rows 3 and 4 of sl st patt. If st gauge is met, garment should be at desired length of 11 (12, 13, 14)". If not, cont in color D in sl st patt until desired length is reached. BO sts for each shoulder or place on st holder for 3-needle BO.

RIGHT FRONT

PU RIGHT front sts from st holder and beg at WS at armhole edge. Cont with stripe sequence at point in which it was placed on st holder. Cont as for back until front measures 9 (10, 11, 12)" from beg. Beg front neck and shoulder shaping.

FRONT NECK AND SHOULDER SHAPING

BO 6 (6, 8, 8) sts at neck edge, work rem 27 (29, 29, 31) sts in est patt. Work shoulder, dec 1 st at neck edge EOR 4 times. Cont in patt to match back. BO 23 (25, 25, 27) sts or place on st holder for 3-needle BO.

LEFT FRONT

PU LEFT front sts from st holder and beg on RS at inside edge, in stripe sequence at point in which it was placed on st holder. Work as for right front, reversing neck and shoulder shaping. Join front and back shoulders.

SLEEVES

Make 2.
Sleeves are worked from the top down. They are not knit in the round, but we recommend using a circular needle. Place markers 4 (4½, 5, 5½)" from shoulder seam on front and back. With RS facing and color D, PU 51 (55, 59, 65) sts evenly between markers. Purl return row. Work rows 1 and 2 of sl st patt in color A, and rows 3 and 4 in color C. With color B, work in St st until sleeve measures 7 (7, 8, 9)" from top. Work sl st patt as follows: Rows 1 and 2 in color D, rows 3 and 4 in color A. With color E, work St st for 2 (4, 4, 4) rows. With color D, work 6 (8, 8, 8) rows in seed st as for stripe 1. Rep color E in St st for 2 (4, 4, 4) rows, dec 13 (13. 17, 19) sts in last row. With color B, work cuff on rem 38 (42, 42, 46) sts, *K2, P2, rep from * for 3 (4, 4, 4) rows. Change to color A, cont in K2, P2 rib for 3 rows. BO in patt.

BUTTON BAND

THIS CARDIGAN is considered appropriate for both boys and girls. To make this garment gender specific, refer to "Buttonholes" on page 13. With RS facing and color C, PU 49 (55, 63, 67) sts along right front edge of garment. Work seed st as for stripe 1 in cardigan body for 5 rows. BO in patt. Rep for left front edge, placing 4 (5, 5, 5) button-holes evenly in 3rd row.

COLLAR

WITH RS facing, beg at right front edge (do not include button band edge) and color D, PU 69 (69, 73, 73) sts as follows: 21 sts to right shoulder seam, 27 (27, 31, 31) sts across back, including sts on st holder, 21 sts from left shoulder seam to left front edge. Cont on collar sts in seed st.

Rows 1 and 2: K2, seed st to last 2 sts, K2.

Row 3: K2, seed st to last 2 sts, inc 1 st, K2.

Rep row 3, working incs into seed st at the end of row just before the last 2 knit sts, until collar measures 1½ (1½, 2, 2)" at ctr back. Change to color E, omit incs, and work in patt for 3 rows. BO sts loosely.

FINISHING

SEW SLEEVE seams and rem side seams together. Place buttons on button band to correspond with buttonholes.

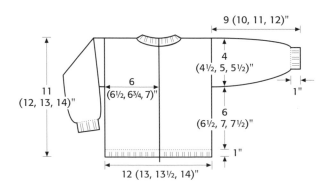

Pants

HONEYCOMB TWEED SLIP-STITCH PATTERN

Row 1 (RS): Color C, K1, *sl 1 wyib, K1, rep from* across.

Row 2 (WS): Color C, purl.

Row 3: Color D, K2, *sl 1 wyib, K1, rep from *, end K1.

Row 4: Color D, purl.

Rep these 4 rows 4 times for 1 pant stripe of 16 rows. With color B, work next 2 rows in St st. This combination of 16-row slip st patt and 2-row color B contrast completes 1 patt stripe. Between leg cuff and beg of waistband, work a total of 7 (8, 8, 9) stripes. All inc and dec are done in color B rows.

LEGS

Make 2.

Cuffs

With color A, CO 54 (62, 66, 74) sts.

Row 1 (WS): *P2, K2, rep from * across row.

Row 2 (RS): *K2, P2, rep from * across row.

Rows 3 and 4: Rep rows 1 and 2.

Row 5: Color B, *P2, K2, rep from * across row.

Row 6: *K2, P2, rep from * across row.

Row 7: Rep row 5.

For sizes 3T and 4T, rep 3 additional rows of ribbing in color B.

Next row: With color D, purl across row inc 1 st at end of row—55 (63, 67, 75) sts.

Schematic measurements:

9 (10, 11, 12)"

4 (4½, 5, 5½)"

11 (12, 13, 14)"

6 (6½, 6¾, 7)"

6 (6½, 7, 7½)"

1"

1"

12 (13, 13½, 14)"

Beg legs.

Beg 4 row honeycomb tweed patt reps and 2 row color B St st for stripes.

Stripe 1: Honeycomb tweed sl st patt for 4 reps over 16 rows. Row 17 (RS): Color B, knit. Row 18: Color B, purl, inc 12 (14, 16, 16) sts evenly in row.

Stripe 2: Rep stripe 1, omitting incs.

Stripe 3: Rep stripe 1, inc 14 sts evenly across row 18.

Rep stripe 1, omitting incs, on 81 (91, 97, 105) sts, until each leg measures 8 (9, 10, 11)" from bottom of cuff. Beg crotch shaping.

CROTCH SHAPING AND BODY

For crotch shaping, next RS row, work in patt across row for one leg. At end of row, CO 4 sts and cont on needle with sts for second leg. At end of row, CO 3 sts, join legs, and place marker for ctr back. Because you are now working in the round, all purl rows in the patt now become knitted rnds. Work stripe 2 on 169 (189, 201, 217) sts until 4 (5, 5, 6) stripes have been completed. Cont in patt on next stripe for 16 rnds; rnd 17, knit; rnd 18, dec 16 (21, 23, 26) sts evenly across rnd. For next stripe, rep 16 rnds of last stripe; rnd 17, knit; rnd 18, dec 18 (23, 23, 26) sts evenly across—135 (145, 155, 165) sts on needle. Work last stripe as for stripe 2 to complete the legs and body of pants.

WAISTBAND

Discontinue knitting in the round at ctr back marker, count around halfway to ctr front, attach color C, and beg waistband rib. Work K1, P1 rib on 135 (145, 155, 165) sts across row. Cont in rib until waistband measures 1½ (1½, 2½, 2½)". BO sts. Front ctr button tab: With color C, PU 13 (15, 15, 17) sts along right vertical open edge of waistband, work in K1, P1 rib for 2 rows. In next row, space 2 (3, 3, 3) buttonholes (YO, K2tog) evenly in row. Work 3 more rows in rib. BO sts.

SHOULDER STRAPS (OPTIONAL)

On top of waistband, space each strap evenly between ctr button opening and side of garment. With desired color, PU 7 sts for each strap and work in K1, P1 rib. Cont until straps are long enough to go over the shoulders, cross in the back, and reach back waistband. Work 3 more rows of rib, place a buttonhole (K2tog, YO) on next row, and work 3 more rows of rib. BO sts.

FINISHING

Sew front legs and crotch to back legs and crotch. Sew buttons on waistband opening to correspond with buttonhole. If applicable, sew button on each side of back waistband for shoulder straps.

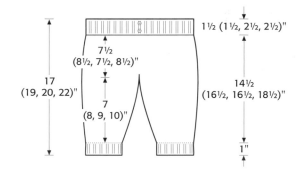

1½ (1½, 2½, 2½)"

7½ (8½, 7½, 8½)"

17 (19, 20, 22)"

14½ (16½, 16½, 18½)"

7 (8, 9, 10)"

1"

123

Acorns Dress

The styling on this dress is one of our favorites. It is splendid on its own, and it's even more adorable when worn in combination with a kid brother dressed in the outfit "Harvest Moon."

This pattern is sized 18M (2T, 3T, 4T).

●

FINISHED MEASUREMENTS

Chest: 22 (24, 26, 28)"
Dress Length: 15 (16, 17, 18)"
Sleeve Length: 2¼ (2½, 2¾, 3)"

MATERIALS

- Tahki Cotton Classic, 50-gram skeins (108 yds), 100% cotton

Color A: 3331 Brown	4 (5, 5, 6) skeins
Color B: 3407 Rust	1 (1, 1, 1) skein
Color C: 3609 Green	1 (1, 1, 1) skein
Color D: 3356 Gold	1 (1, 1, 1) skein

- Size 6 circular needle (24")
- Stitch holders
- Medium-sized crochet hook
- 2 leather buttons, ⅝" diameter (garment buttons shown are by JHB)
- Yarn needle

GAUGE

22 stitches and 28 rows = 4" in pattern stitch. To save time, always check your gauge. If necessary, change needle size to obtain correct gauge.

DRESS SKIRT

THIS SKIRT is knit in the round until the waistband. With color A, CO 240 (264, 288, 312) sts. Place marker to designate beg of rnd, and join ends.

Rnd 1: Purl.
Rnds 2–5: Knit.
Rnds 6–11: Beg checkerboard patt (see graph 1 on page 126).
Rnds 12–16: Color A, knit.
Beg acorn patt (see graph 2 on page 126), placing 20 (22, 24, 26) reps around skirt. After acorns are finished, cont knitting rnds until skirt measures 8½ (8¾, 9, 9½)".
Next rnd: K2tog around. Divide sts for back and front. Place 60 (66, 72, 78) sts on st holder for bodice back. Work rem 60 (66, 72, 78) sts for bodice front.

BODICE FRONT

WITH RS facing:

Rows 1 and 3: K0 (1, 0, 1), *K3, P1, rep from *, end K0 (1, 0 1).
Rows 2 and 4: P0 (1, 0, 1), *P3, K1, rep from *, end P0 (1, 0 1).
Rep these 4 rows until garment measures 13 (13½, 14, 14½)". Beg front neck and shoulder shaping.

FRONT NECK AND SHOULDER SHAPING

WORK IN patt across 20 (22, 24, 26) sts, place ctr 20 (22, 24, 26) sts on st holder. Join second ball of yarn and work rem 20 (22, 24, 26) sts in patt. Work both shoulders in patt, dec 1 st at neck edge every row 4 times. Cont in patt until garment measures

15 (16, 17, 18)". BO 16 (18, 20, 22) sts for each shoulder or place on st holders for 3-needle BO.

BACK BODICE

PU STS from st holder. Work as for bodice front, omitting front neck shaping. Cont until garment measures 13 (14, 15, 16)". Beg back button opening. Divide sts into 2 sections—30 (33, 36, 39) sts each. Join second ball of yarn and work both sections in patt until garment measures 15 (16, 17, 18)". BO 16 (18, 20, 22) sts for each shoulder or place on st holder for 3-needle BO. BO rem back neck 14 (15, 16, 17) sts each side. Join front and back shoulders.

SLEEVES

Make 2.
Sleeves are knit from the top down. They are not knit in the round, but we recommend using a circular needle. Place markers 4 (4½, 5, 5½)" from shoulder seam on front and back. With RS facing, PU 44 (50, 55, 60) sts evenly between markers. Work in St st until sleeve measures 1¼ (1½, 1¾, 2)". On next row, dec 10 (10, 12, 12) sts evenly across row. Change to colors B and C, and work 4 rows of checkerboard patt (same as for border of dress). Work across next row in color A. BO sts.

NECK EDGING

WITH RS facing and color A, beg at back opening, PU 72 (80, 90, 98) sts including sts on st holders. Work 8 rows in St st. BO loosely, letting neck roll over.

FINISHING

SEW ARM and side seams. With color A, single crochet around back opening, creating 2 button loops by making a 1¾" chain at the proper locations on the back opening—one at top of neck and another 1" lower. Make a loop with the chain and secure

onto placket. Repeat for second buttonhole loop and cont around opening. With color D, single crochet around skirt hem. Lightly block dress.

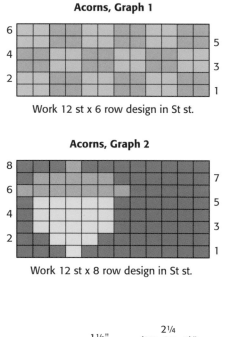

Acorns, Graph 1

Work 12 st x 6 row design in St st.

Acorns, Graph 2

Work 12 st x 8 row design in St st.

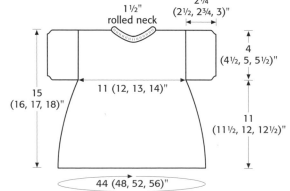

Ja Makin' Me Crazy Dress

𝒲ild, funky, and fun, this crazy sundress is a showstopper. You will love this garment—it doesn't have seams! We made it to button up both sides and to lap the shoulder straps on top with buttons. It begs for sun, sand, and surf.

- Size 5 circular needle (24") for bodice
- Size 6 circular needle (24") for skirt
- Stitch holders
- Medium-sized crochet hook
- 14 (14, 16, 18) buttons, ½" diameter

GAUGE

25 STITCHES and 36 rows = 4" in slip-stitch pattern. To save time, always check your gauge. If necessary, change needle size to obtain correct gauge.

STITCH PATTERNS

Pattern 1: Slip Stitch for Skirt Stripes 1, 3, 5, and 7
Multiple of 8 sts plus 6
(Follow chart on page 129 for all color changes.)
Rows 1 and 3 (RS): Knit.
Rows 2 and 4 (WS): Purl.
Rows 5, 7, and 9: K2, *sl 2 wyib, K6, rep from *, end sl 2, K2.
Rows 6, 8, and 10: P2, *sl 2 wyif, P6, rep from *, end sl 2, P2.
Rows 11, 12, 13, and 14: Rep rows 1–4.
Row 15: Knit.
Row 16: Knit.

Pattern 2: Slip Stitch for Skirt Stripes 2, 4, 6, and 8.
Multiple of 8 sts plus 6
(Follow chart on page 129 for all color changes.)
Rows 1 and 3 (RS): Knit.
Rows 2 and 4 (WS): Purl
Rows 5, 7, and 9: K6, *sl 2 wyib, K6; rep from *.
Rows 6, 8, and 10: P6, *sl 2 wyif, P6; rep from *.
Rows 11, 12, 13, and 14: Rep rows 1–4.
Row 15: Knit.
Row 16: Knit.

Work rows 1–16 in color sequence and patt sequence for each stripe as indicated in chart on page 129.

This pattern is sized 2T (3T, 4T, 6).

●

FINISHED MEASUREMENTS

Total Dress Length: 18½ (20, 22½, 24½)"
Hem to Waist: 11 (11, 12½, 14)"
Bodice Length: 7½ (9, 10, 10½)"
Bodice Width: 22 (23, 24, 26)"

MATERIALS

- Patons Grace, 50-gram skeins (136 yds), 100% cotton

  Color A: 60438 Fuchsia   2 (2, 2, 2) skeins
  Color B: 60604 Terracota   2 (2, 2, 2) skeins
  Color C: 60702 Lime   1 (1, 1, 1) skein
  Color D: 60625 Sungold   1 (1, 1, 2) skeins
  Color E: 60724 Teal   2 (2, 2, 2) skeins

	Color for Rows 1–4	Color for Rows 5–10	Color for Rows 11–14	Color for Rows 15 and 16	Pattern
Stripe 1	B	C	B	A	Patt 1
Stripe 2	D	E	D	B	Patt 2
Stripe 3	A	C	A	D	Patt 1
Stripe 4	B	E	B	A	Patt 2
Stripe 5	D	C	D	B	Patt 1
Stripe 6	A	E	A	D	Patt 2
Stripe 7	B	C	B	A	Patt 1
Stripe 8	D	E	D	B	Patt 2

SKIRT BACK

THE SKIRT is not knit in the round, but we recommend using a circular needle. With size 6 needle and color A, CO 118 (126, 134, 142) sts. Work rows 1–7 to form picot hem for bottom edging.

Rows 1, 3, and 5 (WS): Purl.

Rows 2 and 6: (RS): Knit.

Row 4: (Turning row) K1, *K2tog, YO; rep from * across, end K1.

Row 7: Purl.

Beg patt 1 with color B, and work rows 1–16 as instructed for stripe 1. Follow stripe and patt chart through the completion of row 14 on stripe 6 (6, 7, 8).

Row 15: Color D (D, A, B), K1, *K2tog; rep from * across, end K1—60 (64, 68, 72) sts.

Row 16: Knit.

Change to size 5 needle for waist and bodice. For waist, work 4 rows of garter st (knit every row) of each color as follows:

Size 2T and 3T: Color A, E, B, C.

Size 4T: Color D, E, B, C.

Size 6: Color A, E, D, C.

All sizes: Knit 2 rows in color A.

To shape armhole, BO 6 sts at beg of next 2 rows—48 (52, 56, 60) sts rem.

BACK BODICE

Rows 1 and 7 (RS): Color E, knit.

Rows 2, 4, and 6 (WS): Purl.

Rows 3 and 5: Knit across, dec 1 st at each end of row.

Row 8: Knit.

This est bodice patt of 7 rows in St st and 1 row in purl. Cont rows 1–8 (without decs) until bodice measures 5½ (6, 6½, 7)" from beg of waist (garter st). Next row, work across 19 (20, 22, 23) sts for shoulder strap, BO 6 (8, 8, 10) sts, join second ball of yarn, and work across rem 19 (20, 22, 23) sts for shoulder strap. Work straps in 8-row bodice patt, dec 1 st at inside edge of strap EOR until 10 (10, 12, 12) sts rem on each shoulder strap. When bodice measures 7½ (9, 10, 10½)" from beg of waist, beg strap extension (used to form a loop through buttonhole in front strap). In reverse St st (purl RS rows, knit WS rows), cont on strap sts for 3". BO sts in purl.

SKIRT FRONT

WORK SKIRT front on size 6 needle as for skirt back, and work front waist on size 5 needle as for back waist.

FRONT BODICE

WITH SIZE 5 needle, work 8-row patt as for back bodice. Work 19 (20, 21, 23) sts in color A, 10 (12, 14, 14) sts in color B, and 19 (20, 21, 23) sts in color A as follows:

Rows 1 and 7 (RS): Knit.

Rows 2, 4, and 6 (WS): Purl.

Rows 3 and 5: Knit and dec 1 st at each end of row.

Row 8: Knit.

Cont in rows 1–8 (without decs in rows 3 and 5). In ctr section, every 8 rows, change colors to sequence as follows: E, D, C, B. Depending on size, not all colors will be used. When bodice measures 5½ (6, 6½, 7)" from beg of garter st waist, beg neck and shoulder strap shaping.

NECK AND SHOULDER SHAPING

NEXT ROW, work across 17 (18, 19, 21) sts, BO 10 (12, 14, 14) ctr sts, join second ball of yarn, and work across rem 17 (18, 19, 21) sts. Work shoulder straps as for front, dec 1 st at inside edge EOR until 10 (10, 12, 12) sts rem. When bodice measures 7 (8½, 9½, 10)" from beg of garter st waist, make a 4-st buttonhole in ctr of front strap. Back strap extension will loop through buttonhole to secure shoulder. (See "Buttonholes" on page 13.) After buttonhole, work 1 row in patt. BO sts in purl.

SIDE BUTTON BANDS

BUTTON BANDS are worked in garter st on each side of front and back sections—total of 4 button bands. Garment shown uses color A for each side of back section and color E for each side of front section. However, feel free to mix or match any of the rem colors for which there is enough yarn. For back section, with RS facing and color A, PU 76 (76, 84, 97) sts along side edge from underarm to top of picot hem. Rows 1–6: Knit. BO sts loosely. Rep for opposite side. For front section, with RS facing, in color E, PU 76 (76, 84, 97) sts along side edge. Knit 3 rows, make 6 (6, 7, 8) buttonholes evenly spaced on (RS) 4th row, placing top and bottom buttonholes 2 sts from top and bottom. See "Buttonholes" on page 13. Knit 2 rows. BO sts loosely. Rep for opposite side.

FINISHING

ON EACH side of skirt back section, sew buttons down side to correspond with buttonholes on each side of skirt front section. Loop back strap extension ends, from WS, through front shoulder slots. Draw through and fold over back strap for desired garment length. To secure shoulder straps, sew button through all layers on RS of strap near end of extension.

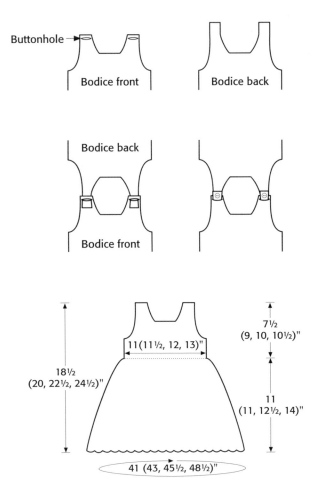

Oui Oui Mademoiselle Dress

For those occasions when you pull out your finery, this elegant dress for the young lady in the family will be stunning. In this dress, styled with a high waist, flowing skirt, and delicate bodice design, she will be the belle of the ball.

FRONT

BACK

This pattern is sized 2T (4T, 6).

•

FINISHED MEASUREMENTS

Bodice Width at Underarm: 22 (24, 26)"
Dress Length: 19 ½ (21 ½, 23 ½)"
Sleeve Length: 3 (3 ½, 4)"

MATERIALS

- Classic Elite Yarns Provence, 125-gram balls (256 yds), 100% mercerized Egyptian cotton

  Color A: 2648 French Blue   2 (3, 3) skeins
  Color B: 2601 White   1 (1, 1) skein

- Size 6 circular needle (24")
- Stitch holders
- Tapestry needle
- Crochet hook
- Approx 1½ yds. of white satin ribbon, ¼"- to ⅜"-wide
- 1 small button, ⅜" diameter

GAUGE

22 STITCHES and 28 rows = 4" in stockinette stitch. To save time, always check your gauge. If necessary, change needle size to obtain correct gauge.

SKIRT

THE SKIRT bottom border is not knit in the round, but we recommend using a circular needle. With color A, CO 265 (281, 305) sts. Beg patt st for bottom border.

Rows 1–3: Beg on WS, knit all 3 rows.
Row 4 (RS): K1, *YO, K2, sl 1, K2tog, psso, K2, YO, K1, rep from * across.
Rows 5 and 6: Purl.
Row 7: Knit.
Row 8: Rep row 4.
Rows 9 and 10: Purl.
Row 11: Purl, dec 17 (17, 17) sts evenly across row. To distribute sts evenly, P2tog every 14 (14, 15) sts. Keep a tally of the number of dec and discontinue when you've dec 17 (17, 17) sts—248 (264, 288) sts.
Row 12: Knit across row. Place marker to designate beg of rnd, and join ends to knit in round. Beg checkerboard patt:
Rnds 1 and 2: Color B, knit.
Rnds 3 and 4: Color A, *K2, sl 2, rep from * around.

Rnds 5 and 6: Color B, knit.

Rnds 7 and 8: Color A, *Sl 2, K2, rep from * around.

Rnds 8 and 9: Color B, knit.

Rnd 10: Color A, knit. (2T only, dec 2 sts in rnd 10—246 sts.)

At marker, est 6 A-line panels as follows: *K39 (42, 46), P2; rep from * around. Work 2 rnds in patt. Next rnd beg A-line shaping. Knit to within 2 sts of the purl sts, work left slant dec (K2tog through back loop), P2, work right slant dec (K2tog through front loop) on next 2 sts. Cont around working left and right slant dec on each side of the P2—a total dec of 12 sts in rnd. Work patt repeating A-line panel shaping every 8th rnd 9 (10, 11) times more—126 (132, 144) sts rem.

Work in patt until garment measures 12½ (14, 15)", ending on WS row. Beg at marker, divide sts for back and front sections. Place back 63 (66, 72) sts on st holder. Work 63 (66, 72) sts for front bodice.

FRONT BODICE

Rows 1, 4, and 5 (RS): Purl.

Rows 2, 6, and 7 (WS): Knit.

Row 3: *K1, YO, K2 (3, 2), sl 1, K2tog, psso, K2 (3, 2), YO, K1, rep from * across.

Cont bodice sts in St st beg with knit row.

Rows 8 and 9: Color B.

Rows 10–12: Color A, inc 0 (1, 1) st in last row.

Rows 13–20: Work bodice graph on 63 (67, 73) sts (see page 134).

Rows 21–24: Color B.

Row 25: K1 (0, 0) in color B, *K1 color A, K2 in color B, rep from * across, ending K1 in color A and, for 2T, last st is K1, color B.

Rows 26 and 27: Color B.

Next 2 (4, 6) rows: Color A.

Next row: P2 (1, 1) sts in color B, *P2 in color A, P1 in color B, rep from * across, end 2T with color A, P1.

Next 2 (4, 6) rows: Color A.

Next 2 rows: Color B.

Cont in color A until front measures 17¾ (19¾, 21)". Beg front neck and shoulder shaping.

FRONT NECK AND SHOULDER SHAPING

With color A, work across 21 (22, 23) sts, cont across 21 (23, 27) sts and place on st holder; work rem 21 (22, 23) sts. Join second ball of yarn, work both shoulders, dec 1 st at neck edge every 4th row 2 times. When front measures 19½ (21½, 23½)", place 19 (20, 21) sts for each shoulder on st holders.

BACK BODICE

Work as for front, omitting front neck shaping. When back measures 18½ (20, 21½)", dec 1 st in ctr of last row. Next row, divide sts equally into 2 sections to create a button placket. Work across 31 (33, 36) sts; place rem 31 (33, 36) sts on st holder. Cont in St st on one section until garment measures 19 (21, 23)". At ctr neck edge, BO 10 (11, 13) sts and work across shoulder sts. Work shoulder sts, dec 1 st at neck edge every row 2 times. When back section measures 19½ (21½, 23½)", BO 19 (20, 21) sts or place on st holder for 3-needle BO. Join yarn and work rem back section, reversing shaping. Join front and back shoulders.

SLEEVES

Make 2.

Sleeves are knit from the top down. They are not knit in the round but we recommend using a circular needle. Place markers 4½ (5, 5½)" from shoulder seam on front and back. With RS facing, PU 48 (54, 62) sts evenly between markers. Purl return row. Next row, K6 (8, 10) sts, inc 1 st in each of the next 36 (38, 42) sts, K6 (8, 10) sts. Cont in St st until sleeve measures 1½ (2, 2½)", ending on WS row. Work 2 rows in color B, 4 rows in color A. Next row, K2tog across row. Next row, purl. Finish sleeve in picot edging in color B as follows:

Rows 1, 3, and 5: Knit.

Rows 2 and 6: Purl.

Row 4: (Turning row) P2, *YO, P2tog, rep from *
across.

BO sts.

NECK EDGING

With color B, work neck in picot edging. With RS facing, start at left back placket edge and PU 64 (70, 80) sts around neck opening. Work edging patt as for sleeves. When completed, leave a tail of yarn to use for button loop.

FINISHING

Sew bottom border seam together. To finish the picot edging for sleeves and neck, fold rows worked after turning row to the WS. Lay the folded section flat against the garment and sew down. Sew side seams and sleeve seams together. With a medium-sized crochet hook and the tail of yarn left at back neck edge, chain 7 sts to make a loop. Pull yarn through at top edge of picot edging and secure tightly. Trim excess yarn. Weave ribbon in open loops through bodice waist. Garment shown has

ribbon tied in the back, but you can also tie the ribbon in front. Sew 1 small button opposite button loop. Steam block garment on wrong side. The skirt should be blocked very, very lightly so as not to flatten the gored skirt. The bodice will respond well to a moderate steaming. Do not block sleeves except to help the picot edging lie flat.

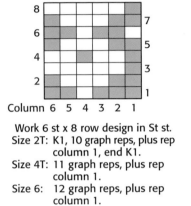

Oui Oui Mademoiselle Graph

Work 6 st x 8 row design in St st.
Size 2T: K1, 10 graph reps, plus rep
column 1, end K1.
Size 4T: 11 graph reps, plus rep
column 1.
Size 6: 12 graph reps, plus rep
column 1.

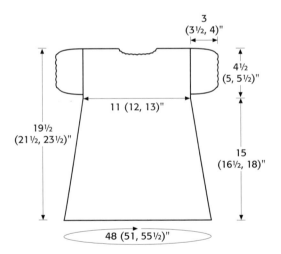

Rosebud Sleeveless Sweater

*I*t's time for tea at the palace and we have just the outfit! Match this easy-to-make fitted cotton sweater with any simple cotton skirt, hat, and gloves.

This pattern is sized 2T (4T, 6, 8).

•

FINISHED MEASUREMENTS

Chest: 22 (24, 26, 28)"
Length: 11 (12, 13, 14)" without ruffle

MATERIALS

- 2 (2, 3, 4) skeins Tahki Cotton Classic, 50-gram skeins (108 yds), 100% cotton, 3446 Pink
- Size 6 circular needle (24")
- Stitch holders
- Medium-sized crochet hook
- Yarn needle
- 1 small rosebud button, ½" diameter (garment button shown is by Dress It Up)

GAUGE

22 STITCHES and 28 rows = 4" in pattern stitch. To save time, always check your gauge. If necessary, change needle size to obtain correct gauge.

BODICE

THIS GARMENT is worked in the round. CO 120 (132, 144, 156) sts. Place marker to designate beg of rnd, and join ends. Work 3 rnds in seed st (see page 20). Beg wide rib st patt.
Rnd 1: Knit around.
Rnd 2: *K3, P1, rep from * around.
Rep these 2 rnds until sweater measures 7½ (8, 8½, 9)". Divide sts for front and back. Place back 60 (66, 72, 78) sts on st holder. Work rem 60 (66, 72, 78) sts for front. Beg armhole shaping.

ARMHOLE SHAPING

WORKING ON front sts, BO 7 (8, 9, 10) sts at beg of next 2 rows. Cont in rib patt, dec 1 st each edge EOR 3 times until front measures 9½ (10, 10½, 11)". Beg front neck and shoulder shaping.

FRONT NECK AND SHOULDER SHAPING

CONT IN patt across 12 (13, 14, 15) sts, BO ctr 16 (18, 20, 22) sts. Join second ball of yarn and cont in patt across rem 12 (13, 14, 15) sts. Work both shoulders in patt, dec 1 st at neck edge every row 4 times. When front measures 11 (12, 13, 14)", BO 8 (9, 10, 11) sts for each shoulder or place on st holder for 3-needle BO.

BACK

PU STS from st holder and work as for front. Join front and back shoulder seams.

RUFFLE

PU 96 (104, 112, 128) sts around hem of garment.

Rnd 1: Knit.

Rnd 2: Knit, inc 2 sts in each st.

Rnds 3–8: *K4, P4, rep from * around.

BO in K4, P4 patt.

FINISHING

SINGLE CROCHET around neck and armhole edges for a nice finish. Sew on decorative button Lightly block garment.

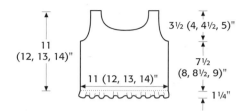

Sassy Swirl Dress

This is an all-around pink favorite for every young girl. See her twirl and swirl with its full ruffled skirt—what fun! The bobbles are after-garment add-ons that can be done in both dress colors or just one of the colors.

This pattern is sized 18M (2T, 3T, 4T).

●

FINISHED MEASUREMENTS

Total Length: 14 (16, 19, 22)"
Bodice Width: 20 (22, 23, 24)"
Bodice Length: 5 1/2 (6 1/2, 7 1/2, 9)"
Sleeve Length: 3 (3 1/4, 3 3/4, 4)"

MATERIALS

- Tahki Cotton Classic, 50-gram skeins (108 yds), 100% cotton
  Color A: 3459 Hot Pink   3 (4, 4, 5) skeins
  Color B: 3001 White   2 (2, 3, 3) skeins
- Size 6 circular needle (24" or 29")
- Stitch holders
- Tapestry needle
- 1 small white button, 3/8" diameter
- 2 yds white satin ribbon, 1/4" wide

GAUGE

22 STITCHES and 28 rows = 4" in stockinette stitch. To save time, always check your gauge. If necessary, change needle size to obtain correct gauge.

SKIRT

WITH COLOR A, CO 440 (480, 520, 540) sts. Do not join ends to work in the round until instructed to do so.
Row 1 (WS): Knit.
Row 2 (RS): Purl
Row 3: Knit.
Place marker to designate beg of rnd, and join ends. Check sts to be sure they are not twisted on needle. Knit 6 (6, 8, 8) rnds. Next rnd, K2tog on all sts to end of rnd—220 (240, 260, 270) sts rem.
Beg skirt rib patt. At marker, *K9, P1, rep from * to end of rnd. Rep in K9, P1 patt until garment measures 7 1/2 (8 1/2, 10 1/2, 12)".
Next rnd: K2tog around on all sts—110 (120, 130, 135) sts rem. Beg waist.
Rnds 1–7: Purl.
Rnds 8 and 9 for 3T and 4T only: Purl 2 more rnds.
Next rnd: Knit. At the completion of this rnd, divide sts for back and front. Place back 54 (60, 64, 68) sts on st holder. Work front bodice on 56 (60, 66, 67) sts.

FRONT BODICE

WITH COLOR B, work K1, P1 across row. Cont in K1, P1 rib until bodice measures 4 (4 1/2, 5 1/2, 6 1/2)", ending on WS row. Beg front neck and shoulder shaping.

FRONT NECK AND SHOULDER SHAPING

CONT IN patt across 19 (20, 22, 23) shoulder sts, BO 18 (20, 22, 21) ctr sts, join second ball of yarn, and cont across 19 (20, 22, 23) sts of second shoulder. Work both shoulders in patt, dec 1 st at neck edge EOR 2 (2, 3, 3) times. When garment measures 14 (16, 19, 22)", BO 17 (18, 19, 20) sts for each shoulder or place on a st holder for 3-needle BO.

BACK

Work sts from st holder, in color B, in K1, P1 rib until back bodice measures 4 (5, 5½, 7)". Divide sts evenly for back neck placket opening. Join second ball of yarn and work on 27 (30, 32, 34) sts for each side of placket opening until garment measures 13½ (15½, 18½, 20½)" from beg. At ctr back edge of each back section, BO 10 (12, 13, 14) sts. Cont on rem 17 (18, 19, 20) shoulder sts until each back section measures 14 (16, 19, 22)". BO sts for each shoulder or place on st holder for 3-needle BO. Join front and back shoulders.

SLEEVES

Make 2.

Sleeves are knit from the top down. They are not knit in the round, but we recommend using a circular needle. Place markers 4 (4½, 5½, 6½)" from shoulder seam on front and back. With RS facing and color B, PU 50 (50, 60, 60) sts evenly between markers. Work in K9, P1 patt (as for skirt) until sleeve measures 2 (2¼, 2¾, 3)". In next RS row, inc 1 st in every 3rd st across row. Work 4 rows in St st. Change to color A, knit 2 rows. BO sts loosely.

COLLAR

Collar is divided in ctr front and is worked in 2 sections. Beg at ctr back opening, with RS facing and color A, PU 45 (52, 59, 59) sts on needle ending at ctr front.

Rows 1–5: Work in St st beg with purl row.
Row 6 (RS): K4, K2tog, YO, *K5, K2tog, YO, rep from * 4 (5, 6, 6) times more, end K4.
Rows 7–10: Work in St st.
BO sts loosely.
Start at ctr front and rep instructions for collar on other side of neck.

FRONT BOBBLES

Bobbles are worked separately and are tied to front bodice in a random manner. Make 18 to 20 bobbles. Bobbles on garment shown are worked in color B. However, either color is suitable. With color B, leaving a 5" tail of yarn, CO 5 sts. K1, P1, K1, P1, K1, and turn. Rep for 4 rows. BO in K1, P1 patt, leaving 5" tail of yarn. Tie yarn tails together tightly to form a ball. Attach randomly to front and tie off tightly on wrong side. Clip threads, leaving a short tail. Do not weave in ends.

FINISHING

Sew sleeve seams and bodice side seams together. Single crochet around back neck opening, creating a small loop for buttonhole. Sew on button to correspond with buttonhole. Weave approx 2 yds of white ribbon through waistband for tie. Tack collar to garment at intervals to stabilize. Block garment lightly.

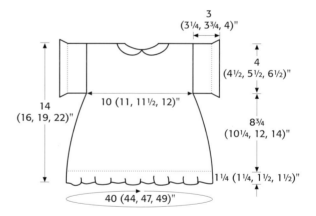

Glossary of Abbreviations and Terms

approx	approximately		**rem**	remain(ing) (s)
beg	begin(ning)		**rep**	repeat
BO	bind off		**rnd(s)**	round(s)
CO	cast on		**RS**	right side of work
cn	cable needle		**sl st**	slip stitch
cont	continue		**ssk**	slip 1 knitwise, slip 1 knitwise,
ctr	center			K2 slipped stitches together through
dec	decreas(e) (ing) (ed)			back loop—1 dec
dpn	double-pointed needle		**st(s)**	stitch(es)
est	establish(ed)		**St st**	stockinette stitch
EOR	every other row		**tog**	together
foll	follow(ing)		**WS**	wrong side of work
inc	increas(e) (ing)		**wyib**	with yarn in back
K	knit		**wyif**	with yarn in front
LH	left hand		**YO**	yarn over needle to make a new stitch
P	purl		**( )**	work directions as a group as many
patt	pattern			times as indicated
psso	pass slip stitch over last stitch worked		*****	starting point for repeating directions
PU	pick up stitches			as many times as indicated
RH	right hand			

Bibliography

Buss, Katharina. *Big Book of Knitting.* New York: Sterling Publishing Company, Inc., 1999.

Walker, Barbara G. *A Treasury of Knitting Patterns.* New York: Charles Scribners's Sons, 1968.

Resources

FOR A LIST of stores in your area that carry the yarns and buttons mentioned in this book, contact the following companies.

YARNS

Berroco, Inc.
14 Elmdale Road
Uxbridge, MA 01569-0367
Wendy Velvet Touch yarns

Cascade Yarns
1224 Andover Park East
Tukwila, WA 98188
Phone: 800-548-1048
Web site: www.cascadeyarns.com
220 and Pastaza yarns

Classic Elite Yarns
12 Perkins Street
Lowell, MA 01854
Phone: 978-453-2837
E-mail: classicelite@aol.com
Provence yarns

Dale of Norway
N16W23390 Stoneridge Drive,
Suite A
Waukesha, WI 53188
Phone: 800-441-3253
Web site: www.dale.no
Freestyle yarns

Patons
1001 Roselawn Avenue
Toronto, Ontario, Canada M6B1B8
Phone: 800-268-3620
Grace yarns

Russi Sales, Inc.
PO Box 4119
Bellingham, WA 98227
Heirloom Easy Care yarns

Skacel Collection, Inc.
PO Box 88110
Seattle, WA 98138
Phone: 253-854-2710
Polo yarns

S.R. Kertzer
105A Winges Road
Woodbridge, Ontario, Canada
L4L6C2
Cotton Connection D.K. No. 2 by Naturally yarns

Tahki • Stacy Charles
1059 Manhattan Avenue
Brooklyn, NY 11222
Tahki Cotton Classic yarns, Filatura Di Crosa Primo yarns

Wool in the Woods
58 Scarlet Way
Biglerville, PA 17307
Phone: 717-677-0577
Web site: www.woolinthewoods.com
Scarlet yarns

BUTTONS AND ZIPPER PULLS

Blumenthal Lansing Company
1929 Main Street
Lansing, IA 52151
E-mail: sales@buttonsource.net
LaMode buttons

Jesse James Button Company
Bethlehem, PA
E-mail: jessejamesco@aol.com
Dress It Up buttons

JHB International
1955 South Quince Street
Denver, CO 80231
Phone: 303-751-8100
Bee, bumblebee, watermelon, silver, Christmas, and leather buttons

Mill Hill
Gay Bowles Sales, Inc.
PO Box 1060
Janesville, WI 53547
Star and Christmas buttons

Trendsetter
16745 Saticoy St. #101
Van Nuys, CA 91406
Phone: 800-446-2425
Cow zipper pull

Zecca
PO Box 1664
Lakeville, CT 06039
Phone: 860-435-2211
Web site: www.zecca.net
Rainbow polymer-clay buttons

About the Authors

Mary H. Bonnette (right), a native of Minneapolis, began knitting at the age of fourteen. She quickly moved from following patterns to creating designs of her own. Mary's work has been featured in ski boutiques throughout Colorado and in many knitting publications. Always artistic, Mary continued designing and knitting throughout her college years. She holds a master's degree in hospital administration. After spending more than twenty years as a healthcare administrator, Mary was inspired to design children's knitwear by the birth of her daughter, Savannah. Now at the age of six, Savannah is learning to knit. Although healthcare has been Mary's career, knitting is her love. She enjoys living in southwest Florida with her husband and daughter, focusing full-time on designing handknit garments for children.

Jo Lynne Murchland (left), originally from West Virginia, began knitting while in college at Denison University. Inspired in childhood by her paternal grandmother, who was an expert seamstress, Jo Lynne learned at an early age to have an appreciation for fabric, fiber, color, and balance of design. She and her husband moved to Florida more than twenty years ago. Prior to 1996, she had worked in both sales and management in the real-estate profession. Knitting has been Jo Lynne's passion for many years. Color, texture, and originality have set her garments apart from the ordinary. Just ask her granddaughters, Ashleigh and Rachel, who will gladly model her creations for any occasion.

In 1995, Mary and Jo Lynne created their own children's knitwear design company, The Sassy Skein. With an emphasis on bold color, creative styling, and kid-friendly comfort, their distinctive garments have been featured in many knitting magazines and by yarn companies. Their first book, *Paintbox Knits* (Martingale & Company, 2001), includes more than thirty delightful designs and has been well received. The charm and pizzazz of their designs will keep knitters in stitches for many years to come!

new and bestselling titles from

Martingale™
& C O M P A N Y

America's Best-Loved Craft & Hobby Books™

That Patchwork Place®

America's Best-Loved Quilt Books®

NEW RELEASES
1000 Great Quilt Blocks
American Stenciled Quilts
Americana Quilts
Appliquilt in the Cabin
Bed and Breakfast Quilts
Best of Black Mountain Quilts, The
Beyond the Blocks
Blissful Bath, The
Celebrations!
Color-Blend Appliqué
Fabulous Quilts from Favorite Patterns
Feathers That Fly
Handcrafted Garden Accents
Handprint Quilts
Knitted Throws and More for the Simply
    Beautiful Home
Knitter's Book of Finishing Techniques, The
Knitter's Template, A
Make Room for Christmas Quilts
More Paintbox Knits
Painted Whimsies
Patriotic Little Quilts
Quick Quilts Using Quick Bias
Quick-Change Quilts
Quilts for Mantels and More
Snuggle Up
Split-Diamond Dazzlers
Stack the Deck!
Strips and Strings
Sweet Dreams
Treasury of Rowan Knits, A
Triangle Tricks
Triangle-Free Quilts

APPLIQUÉ
Artful Album Quilts
Artful Appliqué
Blossoms in Winter
Easy Art of Appliqué, The
Fun with Sunbonnet Sue
Sunbonnet Sue All through the Year

BABY QUILTS
Easy Paper-Pieced Baby Quilts
Even More Quilts for Baby
More Quilts for Baby
Play Quilts
Quilted Nursery, The
Quilts for Baby

HOLIDAY QUILTS
Christmas at That Patchwork Place®
Christmas Cats and Dogs
Creepy Crafty Halloween
Handcrafted Christmas, A
Welcome to the North Pole

LEARNING TO QUILT
Joy of Quilting, The
Nickel Quilts
Quick Watercolor Quilts
Quilts from Aunt Amy
Simple Joys of Quilting, The
Your First Quilt Book (or it should be!)

PAPER PIECING
40 Bright and Bold Paper-Pieced Blocks
50 Fabulous Paper-Pieced Stars
For the Birds
Quilter's Ark, A
Rich Traditions

ROTARY CUTTING
101 Fabulous Rotary-Cut Quilts
365 Quilt Blocks a Year Perpetual Calendar
Around the Block Again
Around the Block with Judy Hopkins
Log Cabin Fever
More Fat Quarter Quilts

TOPICS IN QUILTMAKING
Batik Beauties
Frayed-Edge Fun
Log Cabin Fever
Machine Quilting Made Easy
Quick Watercolor Quilts
Reversible Quilts

CRAFTS
300 Papermaking Recipes
ABCs of Making Teddy Bears, The
Creating with Paint
Handcrafted Frames
Painted Chairs
Stamp in Color
Stamp with Style

KNITTING & CROCHET
365 Knitting Stitches a Year Perpetual
    Calendar
Clever Knits
Crochet for Babies and Toddlers
Crocheted Sweaters
Irresistible Knits
Knitted Shawls, Stoles, and Scarves
Knitted Sweaters for Every Season
Knitting with Novelty Yarns
Paintbox Knits
Simply Beautiful Sweaters
Simply Beautiful Sweaters for Men
Too Cute! Cotton Knits for Toddlers
Ultimate Knitter's Guide, The

Our books are available at bookstores and your favorite craft, fabric, and yarn retailers. If you don't see the title you're looking for, visit us at **www.martingale-pub.com** or contact us at:

1-800-426-3126

International: 1-425-483-3313

Fax: 1-425-486-7596

E-mail: info@martingale-pub.com

For more information and a full list of our titles, visit our Web site.